CROWDFUNDING FOR SOCIAL GOOD

CROWDFUNDING FOR SOCIAL GOOD

FINANCING YOUR MARK ON THE WORLD

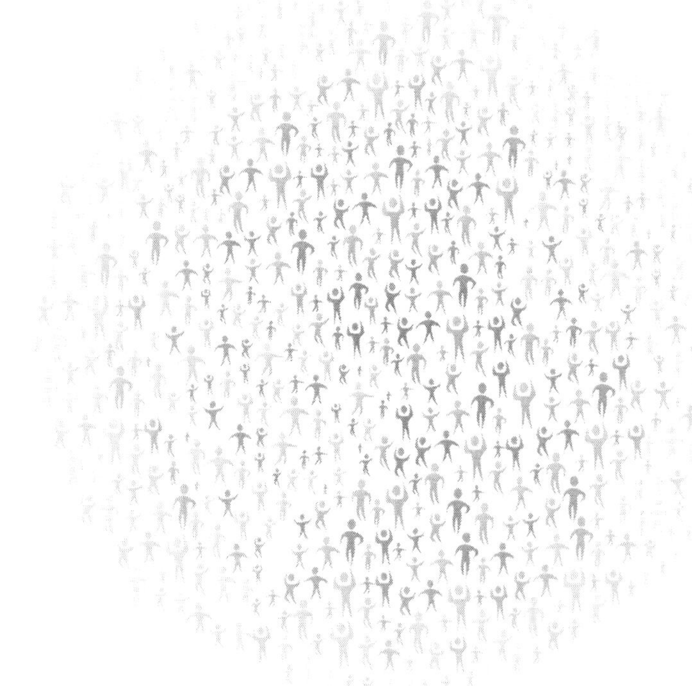

DEVIN D. THORPE

Crowdfunding for Social Good: Financing Your Mark on the World

ISBN: 1491215739
ISBN-13: 978-1491215739

ALSO BY DEVIN D. THORPE

Your Mark on the World: Stories of service that show us how to give more with a purpose without giving up what's most important.

925 Ideas to Help You Save Money, Get Out of Debt and Retire A Millionaire So You Can Leave Your Mark on the World.

Devin's books are available at most on-line retailers, including Amazon.com (amzn.to/2lkCBn) and BarnesandNoble.com (bit.ly/166eM4).

ACKNOWLEDGEMENTS

As my fourth book, I anticipated that writing this book would be relatively easy. Nothing could be further from the truth. The difficulty of writing the book highlights for me the value of the help I've received in the research and writing.

In order to write the book, I've spoken with dozens of people and organizations that have completed successful crowdfunding campaigns. Ultimately, I chose ten stories; I wish there were space to devote to all of those who were willing to share their insights with me.

I am grateful to Jennifer Windrum, Jimi Hunt, Rebecca Pontius, Martha Griffin, Benjamin Cohen, Kaden Benoit, Cason Crane, Muhammed Chadhry, Vivienne Harr, Eric Harr and Dave McMurtry for the time they took to share their stories and for the insights and wisdom they offered.

Jae Dansie edited the book for me. She is a brilliant writer and editor and I am grateful for the outstanding job she did of polishing my prose. Of course, the errors that remain in the book are my responsibility and not hers.

John T. Child created a brilliant cover for my book, as he's done for all of my books.

Gail Thorpe, my wife, has made the greatest sacrifices for this book, not only allowing me time to write, but serving rather formally as proofreader. I am the luckiest man alive.

Despite the help I've received from so many people, any errors that remain in the text are my responsibility alone.

In order to fund the publication and promotion of this book, as seems only fitting, I did a crowdfunding campaign on StartSomeGood.com (bit.ly/hu2WVF). Over 50 people supported the campaign helping me to raise over $3,000 to help me get this book into the hands of real change agents who will use its principles to leave a mark on the world.

The following people supported my campaign at the financial levels indicated:

$499 and up

Jason Best
Crowdfund Capital Advisors
http://crowdfundcapitaladvisors.com (bit.ly/T11RVj)
Raising money isn't easy. But crowdfunding makes it easier than ever before. Success with Crowdfunding has created an educational series that is your key to crowdfunding success. Visit SuccessWithCrowdfunding.com.

Anonymous

$299 and up

Joy Schoffler
Leverage PR
http://www.leverage-pr.com (bit.ly/10aalbD)
The Leverage PR team is unbeaten in the crowdfunding space; no one knows the people, products and platforms better. –*Devin Thorpe*

Doug Ellenoff
Ellenoff Grossman and Schole
www.CrowdESQ.com (bit.ly/1cAgyEZ)
Recognized as a thought leader and expert on the legalities of the JOBS Act, he's been a key representative and advocate for crowdfunding.

Sydney Armani
CrowdFundBeat
http://crowdfundbeat.com (bit.ly/18VIukr)
Crowdfundbeat.com is an online source of news, information and resources for crowdfunding.

John Child
The Brainchild Company
http://johntchild.com (bit.ly/11Fkz6H)
Marketing to the Core: The 4 key concepts that will create results for your small business marketing efforts.

$99 and up

David Bradford
HireVue
http://www.HireVue.com
(bit.ly/SU0ib)
HireVue is a way to interview on demand! Simply email a link to questions and empower candidates to record responses via webcam.

Chris Camillo
Author, *Laughing at Wall Street*
http://laughingatwallstreet.com
(bit.ly/tMvYYI)
In 2007, in the midst of the worst financial crisis since the Great Depression, Chris invested $20,000 and grew it to just over $2 million.

$49 and up

Anonymous

Rick and Alta Davis
The Cystic Fibrosis Foundation
http://www.cff.org (bit.ly/E0B0u)

Andy Kristian Agaba
Hiinga
http://hiinga.org (bit.ly/PGYD7t)

Donald Rands
The Cystic Fibrosis Foundation
http://www.cff.org (bit.ly/E0B0u)

Jane Wolfe
Mardi Gras Throws for Education
http://ubuntuatwork.org
(bit.ly/1X2W1v)

Pearl Wright
Choice Humanitarian
www.choicehumanitarian.org
(bit.ly/jfO4Gt)

$19 and up

Anonymous

Bridgett Thorpe

David M.

John Holt
Utah Microenterprise Loan Fund

Victoria Mita
FundMyTravel

Paul Joseph
Caring Voice Coalition, Inc.

Abe Carter

Alex Budak
Start Some Good

Bill Aho

Cheryl Snapp Conner
Snapp Conner PR

Dave Boyce
Fundly

David Sheffield
Miles of Gratitude

Dyanne Christensen

Evan Malter

J. Todd Anderson
Boy Scouts of America

Kevin Jessop

Anonymous
Tomorrow's Luminary Foundation

Mikey Leung

Rose Spinelli
Animal Protection

Stephen Scott

Steve Grizzell
Girl Scouts of Utah

Nicole Pitzer
Stone by Stone Moving Mountains in Haiti, Inc.

Tom Dawkins
Start Some Good

Wayne Moorehead

$4 and up

Sandy Darlington
Suzanne Rajkumar
Anonymous
Todd Leishman
Devan Thorne
Caroline Udall
Raymond Sweger
Andrew Gardiner
Asha Aravindakshan
Dayton
Franci Eisenberg
Gail Thorpe
Greg Gunn
Kushaan Shah
Leonardo Hudson
M.Cole Jones

For all of the people who dream about leaving a mark on the world, with greatest appreciation for those who actually do.

TABLE OF CONTENTS

Addenda

FOREWORD

Good is a currency.

It is an intangible currency that all humans must embrace; and it is embraced when you discover your definitive purpose in life.

Devin Thorpe is one of the humans I know on this planet that has discovered his definitive purpose in life and has chosen to embrace it, learn it, live it and give it with all of his being.

I noticed this definitive focus when I first met Devin at one of our Kingonomics Innovation, Entrepreneurship and Investment Conferences in Atlanta, GA.

At Kingonomics, we encourage our entrepreneurs and investors to embrace the reality that innovation, entrepreneurship and social good (or investment) is apart of our God given make up. I would argue that it is in our DNA. It's a fundamental construct of our focused existence.

Simultaneously, we expose our audience to the economic philosophies and ideals of Dr. Martin Luther King, Jr. of which we make the case for in my latest book, *Kingonomics: Twelve Innovative Currencies for Transforming Your Business & Life: Inspired by Dr. Martin Luther King, Jr.*

That's correct! Dr. King was very much so focused on economics as his last cause before being silenced by an assassin's bullet in Memphis, TN while marching for fair salaries and benefits of black sanitation workers was the Poor People's Campaign. Dr. King realized that the basis of human, social and civic dignity was human, social and civic good. As you may envision, social good was inherit to Dr. King's DNA. He spoke it. He taught it. He lived it. He breathed it. He manifested it. He died for it.

To do good is to take action. Social investment is action. Crowdfunding is simply the mechanism (or platform) by which we collectively take action to empower the causes and initiatives that we individually, but collectively, are passionate about. As Devin demonstrates with his stories and case studies in his book, Crowdfunding allows us to more together than we can apart.

Upon reading Devin's latest work, *Crowdfunding For Social Good: Financing Your Mark On The World*, I quickly realized that this work is what we called, "Applied Kingonomics". *Kingonomics,* the written prose, is my response to Dr. King's last book, *Where Do We Go From Here: Community or Chaos*. Kingonomics, the conference, boot camps, crowdfunding and wealth building initiatives designed to engage and activate community and culture is what we define as "Applied Kingonomics".

To this end, by reading and embracing the information, strategy and solutions presented in Crowdfunding For Social Good, you'll learn how to take action – through crowdfunding - in your local and global communities by giving, donating and investing.

We will do more together than we will apart.

Devin, well done.

+ Rodney S. Sampson, MBA
Chairman, Opportunity Fund | Hub | CDC
Head of Diversity & Inclusion, One Three Media, Executive Producers of Shark Tank, The Voice, Survivor and Celebrity Apprentice
Author, *Kingonomics: Twelve Innovative Currencies for Transforming Your Business & Life, Inspired by Dr. Martin Luther King, Jr.*

CHAPTER 1

INTRODUCTION

Crowdfunding for Social Good is about helping you to finance your mark on the world as a social entrepreneur.

ARE YOU A SOCIAL ENTREPRENEUR?

You are a social entrepreneur if your focus in building something is to make the world a better place and that takes priority over making a fortune—even if it isn't more important than making a living. It doesn't matter whether you are working out of your basement or hoping to create a global movement, you are a social entrepreneur if your need to help other people exceeds your greed.

If you are a social entrepreneur, the business you run might be called a social venture or social enterprise. Increasingly, such businesses are built with a sustainable, for-profit business model rather than a not-for-profit approach.

Traditional non-profit leaders are also social entrepreneurs. Anyone who seeks to use innovation and enterprise in any form to do good is a social entrepreneur.

Let me encourage you not to get too hung up on the distinctions between for-profit and not-for-profit social enterprises. All businesses, regardless of their tax status or organizational structure must be profitable in order to persist. The only meaningful distinction between for-profit social enterprises and not-for-profit social enterprises is that generally a for-profit business can hope to get all of its revenue from its customers; a not-for-profit business typically requires donations from people other than those served to generate revenue.

WHAT IS CROWDFUNDING?

Crowdfunding isn't just a new name for fundraising. It represents a modern iteration for fundraising unlike any in the past. Crowdfunding is the opposite of soliciting grants from foundations, corporations and governments. Instead it represents your ability to access money from your network—not just the people you know, but the people known by the people you know—and so on. Your network, in its extreme definition, could include every living person. You've probably heard that with no more than six hops from friend to friend that you can reach anyone on the planet.

There are four basic models for crowdfunding being used today, though some are not implemented, as of this writing, in the U.S.

1. **Donations:** These are campaigns that offer virtually nothing in exchange for the money except a promise to carry out a stated charitable purpose, like feeding orphans or saving whales.

2. **Rewards:** Many causes offer rewards, ranging from thank you letters from the people served to new products. Bands use crowdfunding effectively by promising copies of the CD to be produced with the money. Independent filmmakers promise copies of the DVD for the film in exchange for the financial support.

3. **Debt:** Though authorized by Congress, regulations have not yet been issued to allow for raising money in exchange for the promise of repayment with interest, but regulations should allow for implementation before the end of 2013.

4. **Equity:** Like debt, equity crowdfunding is awaiting regulations from the Securities and Exchange Commission and the Financial Industry Regulatory Authority.

Crowdfunding is proving to be a highly successful means of funding a startup even without debt and equity crowdfunding. Rather famously, Pebble, a startup that created a watch that connects with your phone, raised over $10 million on crowdfunding site Kickstarter by taking money for future delivery of the product. The watches shipped in January 2013 (about four months later than promised) after completing the crowdfunding campaign in May 2012.[1]

Most crowdfunding campaigns, however, raise much less. Brian Meese and Jed Cohen, founders of Rockethub, a crowdfunding site based in New York City, explained that the typical campaign raises $3,500 to $35,000 across all platforms. Equity based campaigns in the UK where crowdfunding for equity is already legal and implemented see an average deal size of $88,000 on the site Crowdcube, suggesting that equity crowdfunding should raise an average of four to twenty times as much as the donations and rewards based models.[2]

WHAT'S THE CONNECTION?

At this point, you may be wondering why write a book about crowdfunding specifically for social entrepreneurs? The answer is simple. Social entrepreneurship and crowdfunding were made for each other. Call it fate, kismet or destiny, but much of the money raised through crowdfunding is for social entrepreneurs.

Crowdfunding is growing so quickly it is likely to become a key part of the fundraising mix for all nonprofits. It could become the

1 http://money.cnn.com/2013/01/09/technology/innovation/pebble-ship-date/index.html (cnnmon.ie/13hEokb)

2 http://www.forbes.com/sites/devinthorpe/2013/01/09/top-ten-issues-raised-at-texas-crowdfunding-conference/ (onforb.es/13hlLuB)

sole source of funding for many social ventures, especially when adding in the debt and equity crowdfunding that will be coming on line later this year.

For traditional nonprofits and new social entrepreneurs with no crowdfunding experience, this book serves as a guide to help you navigate this new territory.

CHAPTER 2

SOMETIMES YOU JUST WANT TO SMAC! CANCER

Jennifer Windrum's life changed when her mother, living half a continent away, was diagnosed with cancer.[3]

In 2005, when Jennifer's mother, Leslie Lehrman, was diagnosed, Jennifer was living in Omaha, Nebraska, while her mother was in Phoenix.

"My Mom is the inspiration behind the creation of SMAC! (bit.ly/Sidr13) She lived more than 1,200 miles away, making her appointments, tests, scan results and treatments that much harder for both of us," Jennifer said. "I wanted to give her something she could have, hold, and touch when I couldn't be with her. I created SMAC! to give Mom (and others) a 'buddy' she could hug to remind her that I am with her."

She was determined to do something to show support for her mother so far away.

3 The information for this chapter was obtained directly from Jennifer Windrum through a series of interviews conducted by email beginning in the fall of 2012 and ending in the spring of 2013.

On one of her visits to see her mom, Jennifer, took two sock monkeys that her own daughters had given her for Mother's Day. Jennifer says, "Mom named the monkeys "Hope" and "Ned" and held them tightly."

Leslie, who never smoked, ultimately succumbed to the lung cancer on December 5, 2012. Her passing has served to further fuel Jennifer's passion to bring comfort to those with/impacted by all types of cancer, as well as increase awareness and funding for lung cancer. She says, "The minute my mom told me she had lung cancer, my mission and path in life became crystal clear. My mom's future became anything but. My mom was far from alone. We literally have a public health epidemic on our hands and virtually no one cares. I won't stand for it. None of us can."

"My social mission is to arm those with or impacted by cancer with SMAC! monkeys (Sock Monkeys Against Cancer) to provide constant, *tangible* love and support throughout their journeys, while at the same time, fostering the gift of giving and contributing to cancer research and programs."

Over the long run, Jennifer plans to give away a SMAC! monkey for every one she sells and to donate some of her profits directly to cancer programs and research.

Jennifer turned to the crowdfunding site StartSomeGood to launch her social enterprise. Drawing on her experience in social media, Jennifer says, "The SMAC! campaign opened with the highest-earning first day in the history of the crowdfunding platform, raising over $5,000 within 24 hours."

StartSomeGood operates with a two-tiered goal structure. You set a "tipping point" threshold that you are required to reach in order to keep your money and a goal that represents the total you'd like to raise. If you don't reach your tipping point threshold, the supporters keep their money and you go home disappointed.

Jennifer set a high goal of $35,000 and a remarkably high tipping point threshold of $27,000—and reached both goals, providing her with the startup money she needed to begin operations. She produced—or as she says—"unleashed" 1,000 SMAC! monkeys with the money.

Jennifer developed her social media strategy well before she launched her crowdfunding campaign. She started by seeking input for ideas from the online community she and her mom built to chronicle her cancer journey and bring together others with lung cancer: "WTF? (bit.ly/5ijCWL) (Where's the Funding) for Lung Cancer?"

In order to connect with the social media generation, soon after her Mom's diagnosis, Jennifer created the "WTF for Lung Cancer" campaign. She explains, "I knew I had to come up with an attention-getting, edgy campaign in order to cut through the clutter." She went on to say, "Lying in bed one night it hit me: The double-meaning of 'WTF?' in today's digital language and 'WTF?' for 'Where's the Funding?' For those who don't know the digital 'WTF?' the message is still clean and simple. For those who get both meanings, it's a double-punch!"

Within the WTF? community, Jennifer crowdsourced a lot of important decisions, such as naming the SMAC! monkey prototypes and determining what colors they should be. So, it was natural for her to then turn to crowdfunding to raise the money.

"I felt that bringing the SMAC! monkeys to life through a community effort was the most natural and appropriate way, " Jennifer says, adding, "Grassroots movements are so powerful and, in my opinion, so much more meaningful."

Jennifer launched the crowdfunding campaign with a party she called a "SMAC!-down." This brilliant step created real-world enthusiasm for her online campaign and must certainly have contributed to her opening day success. She livestreamed the event over the web and encouraged people to host similar parties in their own homes—which many did. She says, "I set up laptops where people could pledge right then and there, while they ate, drank and mingled." She noted that this was a great way to include people who are not comfortable in the online arena "and only write checks."

A key part of Jennifer's strategy was building an army online. In addition to the WTF? community, Jennifer created a private group of "ambassadors" on Facebook that was able to watch, and be part of, the creation of the SMAC! monkey prototypes from beginning to end. These "SMAC!-ers," as Jennifer calls them, were fully invested in the project and wanted to be part of helping the campaign become a success.

Of the future, Jennifer says, "I truly want to create a SMAC! monkey revolution, where a SMAC! monkey instantly becomes top-of-mind as a true "creature comfort" for someone with or impacted by cancer." She continued, "Each major type of cancer will have its own custom monkey. My dream is to get cancer centers on board to give SMAC! monkeys to their patients."

LESSONS LEARNED

When I asked Jennifer about the lessons she learned from crowdfunding, she noted that you need to "expect the unexpected." Some of the people you think you can count on, won't be there for you. On the other hand, she says, "complete strangers came out of the woodwork wanting to help in big ways and small."

She also reiterated the "power of community." She noted that it was this community of real people that came together to make her success possible.

CHAPTER 3

GOAL ASSESSMENT: CAN YOU GET THERE FROM HERE?

As you think about crowdfunding, you risk falling into a painful trap. If you fixate on the crowdfunding campaigns that have raised millions of dollars, you risk being disappointed. As noted in the introduction, most campaigns raise between $3,500 and $35,000. Figuring out where your campaign has the potential to go is a critical first step.

YOUR CAUSE

Not all causes will resonate in the same way, even with your close friends. If you hope to create a for-profit venture with a social mission attached, you will likely need to offer greater rewards or raise equity or debt. Even among nonprofits, the appeal of each nonprofit project varies. No one ever gave a donation to a cause just for the tax benefit.

Consider the following issues. For each one, give yourself a score on a scale from one to five with one representing a poor score and five being perfect. At the end, you can assess your cause overall. Your campaign's success does not depend entirely on any single factor or even on your cause taken as a whole.

Face: Think about the face of your campaign. If you can immediately think of the image you would use as the face of your campaign it increases the cause's appeal. For instance, if you can think of an actual child that would be symbolic of your campaign, do it. A cuddly critter could work well, too. Images of almost any person will be better than images of buildings, landscapes, or places. Have a logical connection between your cause and the face you choose in order for that face to be effective. For instance, if you use the face of a poor child in a campaign to help mitigate the effects of climate change, you must be able to draw a clear connection between the poor child and your campaign. If your campaign won't make the child tangibly better off than she is today, you have probably stretched too far.

Urgency: Consider the extent to which people will naturally react emotionally to your cause. This can be the case following a disaster like the earthquake in Haiti or Hurricane Sandy. The more tragic and sudden the problem, the more emotional appeal it will have. Raising money for disaster relief immediately after the disaster is easier than it is to raise money for permanent problems like poverty and disease because of the emotional connection people feel to the current event.

Politics: Politically charged campaigns cut both ways. Issues like abortion and gay rights can be divisive but also catalyze action among people who already feel passionately about issues. Generally, however, the more divisive the issue the harder the campaign will be. Not only will some people choose not to give to your campaign, even those who do may not be as willing to advocate for your campaign. Give yourself a high score on this measure if your cause is not politically divisive.

Geography: While there is some romantic appeal to faraway places like the Congo and Cambodia, if your cause is local and will benefit people right in your own community—people you know and that your friends know—you are likely to have more success. Score yourself higher for local projects, lower for projects in distant but impoverished places, and lowest of all for projects in well-developed areas that are far from home, whether across the country or on the other side of the world.

Community: If you are already a part of a certain community that will naturally connect to your cause, that bodes well for your campaign. For instance, if you are a member of Rotary and you are raising money for a project supported by your local Rotary club, you have a community that you can appeal to with your campaign. And not just your local club, but potentially all Rotarians.

Project or Event: Campaigns work best when there is a project or an event associated with them. You can fabricate an event, if there isn't one naturally. If you are raising money for your group to complete a discrete humanitarian project within a specific time frame to remedy an acute problem, you have the ideal situation for crowdfunding. On the other hand, if you are raising money for an ongoing project, you may need to identify or create an artificial event such as using a holiday or other calendar event to serve as a goal.

Once you have graded your cause using the five-point scale on all six of the above criteria, you should have a score to help guide you in your thinking. The higher the score, the more likely it is that people outside of your network engage in your campaign. The lower your score, the less likely they are to donate or campaign for you.

TEAM

Now that you've assessed your cause, let's assess your team. If you are doing this all alone, give some thought to how you might build a team.

Crowdfunding is a numbers game. The more people you have at the center of your network the bigger the network and the more successful the campaign is going to be. Not everyone on your team will contribute in the same way. Your team will be effectively made up of *partners*, *champions*, and *boosters*.

A partner, in this sense, is someone who is formally involved in the project—perhaps literally a partner in a startup business. These people would also include employees have agreed to work closely with you on the crowdfunding campaign. But all employees are not necessarily partners.

Champions include people outside the partner circle who have agreed to help champion the campaign. While champions talk a good game, not all of them will work as actively as others. A champion is someone who has formally committed to help.

Boosters are fans and friends you think you can count on to help, but who have not formally committed to work on the campaign. With luck, you'll identify boosters early and help them to be effective. Some will prove to be more productive in spreading the word and raising money than your champions. Among your close friends and volunteers, you may likely count on one out of 100 to become boosters.

While everyone on the team will vary in effectiveness for a variety of reasons, as a rough guide to money, you and your partners may each be able to attract $2,000. Your champions could average $1,000 each. Finally, your boosters could raise $500 apiece. To complete the example, if you have three partners, including yourself, five champions and you hope to find five more boosters, your campaign could reasonably hope to raise $13,500 ($2,000 x 3 + $1,000 x 5 + $500 x 5 = $13,500). You can quickly see the value in building a formal team before you launch.

YOUR NETWORK

The next key thing to assess is your network, friends, family, colleagues, fans, supporters, and others you know that you are comfortable contacting with your campaign.

As you think about the relevant network, it would include the personal networks of all of the people who are partners in the project. The people who will be working actively on the project day-to-day, and who are fully committed to use their networks to raise money for the project, are those whose networks you'll want to assess. There are several criteria you should measure for each partner: the number of people you will each call on the phone, email, and contact through Facebook, Twitter or other social network.

ASSESSING EACH PARTNER'S NETWORK

People you will phone: Each partner on the team should write down the names of all of the people he or she is willing to call for help with the campaign. You'll each need to consider not only your relationship with people, but also the time required to make calls. Only put someone on your call list if they are more likely than not to contribute to your campaign or at least help promote it. (You will likely overestimate the likelihood of their participation, but that's okay for now.)

People you will email: Additionally, you should each dump your full email Rolodex into a spreadsheet and identify the number of people you are willing to email for your campaign. You'll want to be careful about spam regulations (both governmental and policies enforced by your email provider). For example, Google won't let you send more than 500 copies of an email. Legitimate email marketing services like Constant Contact and MailChimp will also purge your lists or deny any further service if too many people mark your email as spam. Only put people on your list who know you. Spamming everyone in your Rolodex may do more harm than good.

Facebook friends: Next, each of you should check the number of your Facebook friends. Those friends likely include some of the people on the lists above, so be sure not to double count. You may share friends in common with your partners, so don't double count those. Facebook is perhaps the most important tool in your campaign, because you can reach the same people over and over again in new ways without offending them—if you do it right. Even still, you are unlikely to get more than one in 100 of your Facebook friends to donate or share your campaign with their friends.

Twitter followers: For most people, Twitter relationships are less formal and intimate than Facebook friends. Most of your followers likely share an interest in something you've tweeted about, but some are only looking to increase their own fan base and follow lots of people only to see if they will follow back. Realistically, you are unlikely to get more than 1 in 1,000 of your twitter followers to contribute to your campaign. Thankfully, more are apt to retweet a tweet about your campaign, but you won't likely get big numbers from Twitter.

Other social networks: There are a host of other social networks. You'll want to engage all of your friends on all of your networks, so be sure to count your friends, followers and fans on any social network to help gain a sense of how much money you can raise.

ESTIMATING YOUR POTENTIAL

Now that you have been through the assessment, let's do some calculations to see if you can make a rough estimate of what your campaign can likely achieve based on what we've learned.

Your Cause: First, let's consider the emotional appeal of your campaign. On the 30-point scale if you scored below 10, you should probably quit now because even your friends will be reluctant to fund your campaign. If you scored between 10 and 20, your campaign will likely not reach beyond the network of the partners. If you scored between 20 and 25, your campaign will likely garner 25 percent of the proceeds from people outside your network. If you scored above 25, your campaign could raise as much as 75 percent of the campaign proceeds from outside your network.

Your Network: In order to determine how much money you can raise from your network, let's consider some standard data from donation-based crowdfunding. You can expect to get about 20 times as much using equity or debt. For donation and reward-based crowdfunding, the most typical contribution is $20. The average across all donations works out to about $75 or $80. Obviously, a few large donors are skewing the data a bit. The best-case scenario for your network would be to get one in ten of the people from all of your lists to donate the average amount. So if you have 1,000 people on all of your lists, you would expect to max out your network at about $7,500 to $8,000.

Campaign: When you combine the implication of your cause score with your network score, you begin to see the potential of your campaign. If your cause score suggests not to expect much beyond your network, then you are already done with the math portion of this exercise. If you can expect to get a total of 25 percent of your money from outside the network, take the estimate of the network and divide by .75, which would yield $10,000 if your network estimate were $7,500. If your cause suggests you can glean 75 percent of your proceeds from outside your network, then divide your network value by .25, which yields $30,000 if your network is potentially going to provide $7,500. Consider a campaign of that size a home run!

Serendipity: There are a few campaigns that achieve much more than their potential according to this assessment. Chalk that up to serendipity. Such campaigns are few and far between. Always hope for the best, but plan your campaign around the numbers in this exercise.

Marketing: Most people will find that the bulk of the money for their campaigns ultimately comes from their network. The success of such a campaign has much more to do with your marketing than your cause or the good-heartedness of your friends. It will take a lot of work and some money to educate everyone in your network about what you're doing and why they should help you do it. If you don't do the work, you will not get the results you want or expect.

CHAPTER 4

LIVE MORE AWESOME

Jimi Hunt says, "I was horribly depressed." He struggled with depression for three years during which he lost his marriage and his job.

He was counseled to set a goal, a challenging goal. He decided to float the 425 kilometer (264 miles) Waikato River in New Zealand where he lives using a $15 "Lilo" float—the sort you might use to soak up the sun in a swimming pool.

One of the problems those with depression face, especially men in New Zealand, Jimi says, is the reluctance to ask for help. So, he asked for and received help all along the way during his river run. Each night a supporter hosted him and in several spots along the river he recruited help from boaters to cross still water.

The 14-day project was a huge success, helping Jimi conquer his depression and yielded an entertaining documentary film, which can be found at www.lilothewaikato.co.nz (bit.ly/odlE1Y). He also developed a great social network following and brought awareness to his cause: helping others to overcome their depression.[4]

4 http://www.lilothewaikato.co.nz/ (bit.ly/odlE1Y)

After the float, Jimi needed an encore. He began plans to construct the world's largest water slide to help him launch an organization he called Live More Awesome that would work to battle depression by bringing attention to it, thereby making it easier for sufferers to ask for help.

Jimi explained that depression in New Zealand is unusually bad, second worst in the OECD. Why depression is so bad in New Zealand no one understands, though Jimi says it may have something to do with the can-do culture, the perception of isolation in the world, and drinking.

Jimi says that because men in New Zealand have a "macho" image and try to deal with things themselves, "our tag line is 'ask for help.'"

To build the water slide, Jimi would need money—a lot of money. The water slide was to be built on the side of a farmer's hill in New Zealand. A record-setting water slide, however, won't build itself. The budget: $35,000.

He felt real pressure as he contemplated how to raise this money. He says, "In New Zealand we have more nonprofits per capita than any country on earth." With such a limited pool, he felt that in order to win, "we have to have better ideas and execute them well. That's how you differentiate yourself from the others out there."

Jimi decided to raise money using IndieGoGo (bit.ly/WTdTLa). He knew he could leverage the social network he'd built during his Lilo trip, but to raise the money he needed, he'd have to reach beyond that network.

One key to his success, Jimi knew, would be a compelling video. He and his team began by watching all of the successful crowdfunding videos he could find on IndieGoGo.

They recognized the video needed to be short and needed to "make people feel something," as well as deliver a message. "We made it ourselves with our friends," Jimi says. "We had people tell their stories in it."

Once the video was ready, they organized the campaign. Jimi's partner, Dan Drupsteen, who also battled depression, helped lead the charge along with an intern from Boston. Together, they developed a comprehensive marketing plan, leveraging Jimi's skills and experience in the marketing industry.

They began by identifying influencers on Klout and inviting them to tweet and post on Facebook about the campaign. Then, they engaged bloggers who wrote about depression. From there they expanded their outreach to include bloggers who write about "awesome things," Jimi explained.

They reached out to the general media, starting with local media. With the local media's help they were successful in building a large local audience.

Finally, with a foundation of local media and bloggers talking about the campaign, the team reached out to the national and international media. "You can't just wait for media," Jimi says. "You have to go out and tell them the story." They got a blogger at the *Huffington Post* to write about the campaign as well as an article in the UK's *Daily Mail*.

The team believed that if they got some international exposure, with big media outlets, lots of local media around the world would cover it. Their experience suggests their plan worked.

Not only did they cover the $35,000 cost of the water slide, but they raised $60,000 more than their target for a total of $94,677.

One of the key messages of the campaign to fight depression, "ask for help," proved to be important for the campaign as well. Jimi secured the biggest billboard in New Zealand for the campaign just by asking.

But everything didn't go perfectly. The fundraising the first two days was disappointing and Jimi feared the campaign might be in trouble before it really even got started. But the media picked up the story and saved the campaign.

One of the lessons Jimi learned during the campaign is that "people are inherently stupid," he says with a good-natured laugh. There was a tremendous amount of work involved in helping people correct the mistakes they made when choosing perks on the IndiGoGo platform. That was work he hadn't anticipated.

The rewards for the campaign were interesting. For a $5 donation, supporters received only thanks. For $10, they were issued a rubber ducky to float down the water slide in their place—a popular perk for people around the world wanting to support the campaign, but who couldn't otherwise participate. The duckies were sent down the slide together. The first ducky to arrive at the bottom was declared the winner and sent to its corresponding donor.

The other rewards generally consisted of access to the slide during its two-day operation in February 2013.

The water slide operation was a huge success. Visit the Live More Awesome Facebook page (on.fb.me/16I24mp) to see the hundreds of photos taken during the event.

One final thought Jimi offered: "If you don't capture their imagination, you won't capture their money."[5]

5 Telephone interview with Jimi Hunt on March 5, 2013.

CHAPTER 5

DESIGNING YOUR CAMPAIGN STRATEGY

A successful crowdfunding campaign takes more time to prepare than it does to run. It is rather like an iceberg in that you can only see about 10 percent of the effort in a successful campaign when you look at what is happening publicly around it. Weeks—if not months—of planning were likely involved, coupled with a lot of behind-the-scenes work during the campaign itself. To a casual observer, it may look like a cute campaign video was posted on a platform and that money just rolled in. To the fundraiser who can see the massive part of the iceberg below the water line, the campaign looks either like a Rube Goldberg contraption or a well-oiled machine.

Your strategy should be organized as a time line, identifying the things you need to do before, during, and even after the campaign is completed. Chances are that a successful campaign is just the beginning of your work.

You'll probably want to break down the work into weeks, with at least six weeks of preparation leading up to a six-week campaign. You'll similarly want to schedule the follow-up across the weeks, making sure that you follow up with your supporters before too long.

There are six special considerations that you'll need to address in your strategic plan. We'll discuss each at length later in the book, but for now here are some highlights to get you thinking about your plan:

1. **Producing a video:** Many people argue that the video is the most important part of a crowdfunding campaign. Some sites require a video in order to post a campaign. Data also shows that campaigns with videos do about twice as well as campaigns without. While you may be able to produce an adequate video in an hour on your laptop, if you are serious about raising tens of thousands of dollars rather than just a few thousand from your friends, plan to invest some time and perhaps some money in creating a first rate video. Allow several weeks for producing the entire video.
2. **Choosing rewards:** Before you launch your campaign, you've got to be strategic about the rewards you'll offer. For some nonprofits, it may be adequate to offer little more than increasingly creative thank-you notes for donations of increasing size. For social enterprises with a profit motive, it may be much more important to offer tangible rewards or products in association with the raise. If you will have to produce or buy these rewards, it may require plenty of planning to be ready to deliver the rewards.
3. **Prelaunch your campaign:** It is important to have key supporters, friends, and family lined up before your first day to pledge at least 10 percent and perhaps as much as 50 percent of your goal. You don't want strangers arriving at your campaign page and finding that no one has donated. Not only will they not donate, they likely won't come back. Everyone wants to be a part of something; your early momentum signals that you have a movement and others will want to join in. Virtually all of your one-to-one campaigning needs to start before you actually launch your campaign.
4. **Marketing the campaign to your network:** Although much of your marketing will happen after you launch your campaign, you want to set out detailed plans for your campaign before you launch. You'll want to know when you're sending email blasts and

to whom, when you are posting on Facebook and Twitter, and so on. You can always change plans during the campaign if something's not working, but you will likely be too frantic during the campaign to think strategically. Be sure to think through whom you'll call, whom you will email and whom you will reach through your social network.

5. **Budgeting for the campaign:** A campaign can be completed for free if you use the right platform and do everything yourself. Most platforms, however, charge a small fee (usually about 5 percent of the money raised). In addition, you may want to budget as much as ten percent more for marketing expenses to cover costs like video production, press releases, and hiring marketing help. Again, you can do this yourself, but adding the reach of professional services can do far more for your campaign in addition to paying for itself.

6. **Build relationships of trust:** In order to get money from people, you have to build a relationship of trust. Think about this: the first people to donate are likely to be the people who know you best. Why? It's because of the relationship of trust. You will want to build your strategic plan to focus specifically on creating trust by establishing your *bona fides* through formal and informal endorsements from others. Marketers call this authenticity. Be real.

By building a week-by-week plan to prepare and execute your campaign, you create the possibility for dramatic success.

CHAPTER 6

DO GOOD BUS ROLLS ACROSS THE COUNTRY FULL OF VOLUNTEERS

Rebecca Pontius and her friend had been volunteering regularly in Los Angeles where she lived and says she was frequently asked, "How do you know where to volunteer? How do you get involved?"[6]

Rebecca Pontius

To a natural volunteer the questions bordered on absurd, but rather than dismiss the questions or answer them in a more traditional way, Rebecca had an idea.

"We decided to put all those questioning friends on a bus and *show* them exactly how to volunteer. Our plan was

6 The information for this story was largely gathered via an online interview on December 10, 2012.

to make it EASY to volunteer and even have a little fun along the way," Rebecca said. "We wanted to take away the frustration of searching online, deciding which non-profit was best or close enough to home... and simply take them right to a cause and let them dive in."

They began doing simple events with their friends, organizing a busload of volunteers for this or that project in L.A. As the success of their efforts grew, they started inviting other Los Angelinos to join them in their efforts.

Then Rebecca and her friends had the really big idea of taking the bus across the country, doing service projects everywhere they went.

They decided to partner with the band Foster the People and follow them around the country.

The challenge was to raise the money to fund a cross-country trip with a bus full of volunteers. At first, they tried to find corporate sponsors, believing that the connection to the popular band, combined with doing good, would be a compelling corporate sponsorship opportunity. "What company wouldn't want massive exposures *and* do good?" Rebecca asked.

Ultimately, the corporate sponsorships weren't coming together quickly enough, so they decided to try raising the money on Kickstarter, the largest crowdfunding site. On the day they were ready to launch, they got kicked off Kickstarter because their project wasn't a creative one.

Needing a new home for their campaign, they began looking for alternatives and found StartSomeGood. They quickly moved the campaign over to the new platform and launched.

Building on their relationships in two communities—the community of volunteers who were actually getting on the buses with them and the fans of Foster the People—they quickly raised over $100,000 to pay for their cross-country, rolling service party.

Rebecca reports, "We did exactly what we planned—we took the Do Good Bus on Foster the People's North American 2011 Summer Tour. We visited 25 cities, helped 25 causes, and met over 750 volunteers."

Rebecca and her friends haven't quit. The Do Good Bus packs in a new batch of volunteers regularly to take them out to volunteer at a surprise location. That's right, the volunteers don't know where they're going until they get there. They believe that making the destination a surprise allows the volunteers to approach each service opportunity with an open mind.

The Do Good Bus (bit.ly/gQdAv6) team now offers corporations ready-made experiences that go beyond traditional, team-building exercises by putting people in a position to have a social impact together.

Their formula for success is: [strangers + bus + do good + fun].

CHAPTER 7

REWARDS THAT INSPIRE

If you are leading a social enterprise, the crowdfunding rewards you choose should not only motivate donations, but also inspire people to become involved.

When you visit a crowdfunding campaign, one of the first things you'll notice are giving levels, which often include a description of a reward or an impact statement. Choosing what you'll say and do is one of the keys to a successful campaign.

It is true that some platforms don't allow you to list rewards with your campaign. That may be the case if you are a nonprofit listing on a site that caters only to nonprofits. There are tax issues that arise as soon as someone receives something of value with a contribution. Even though you may not be able to offer financially valuable rewards, you may be able to offer creative ways to say thank you that not only inspire people to give, but also to spread the word—which could be even more valuable.

At a minimum, even for nonprofit social ventures, you'll want to offer a cascading level of thank-you notes and recognitions. Most platforms will provide a way for you to set up an automated thank-you note and receipt. You may also want to tweet a thank-you to everyone who provides you with a Twitter handle.

Perhaps more important than the thank-you and recognition for nonprofits would be the impact statement you make for each level of giving. When it makes sense to do so, be sure to note the good you can do with the donation. Something like, "Your $25 gift provides a family with access to clean water for life." If you can't match a gift to a specific outcome like that, you could say, "Your gift of $25 brings us closer to our goal of curing childhood cancer."

You can also provide recognition on your website or at an event associated with your campaign. Donors at a $500 level could receive much greater recognition than your $50 donors, but all could still be listed. At an event, one possibility is to hang banners in prominent places to recognize major donors.

Walk through any university building in America, and you'll see that it is full of recognition for donors who helped to build the building, classrooms, study rooms, and specialty rooms. You may even find a brick wall with names on each brick for "small" donors who gave $500 or $1000. The "naming rights" for the building, the rooms in the building, the equipment in the building, the chairs in the rooms, likely exceed the cost of constructing the building—the university needed to raise money for an endowment to maintain the building properly. Think as creatively as a university dean about how you'll recognize your donors.

Beyond thank-you notes and recognition, your nonprofit may wish to offer some perks or rewards to inspire people to give or give more. Remember our friend Jimi Hunt in New Zealand who built a water slide to support his cause of fighting depression and suicide in his homeland—an epidemic problem there. He raised money globally by promising to send a rubber ducky with each donor's name written on the bottom down the water slide. He filmed and posted the "event" for all to see. Only the first ducky down the slide—who was rightfully declared the winner—was actually sent to the donor. The rest simply got to participate in the event by ducky proxy.

As one of the more clever examples of rewards was offered by a nonprofit called Arcas working to protect sea turtles. They incubated eggs and then released the hatchlings. Their reward was to video the hatchling scurrying into the ocean across the donor's name written in the sand. Clever and topical, this reward provides a personal connection between the donor and the beneficiary, providing them a Facebook-worthy thank-you.

Many social entrepreneurs use t-shirts, posters, and bumper stickers as low cost rewards. These can work well for nonprofits if offered at high-enough donation levels that the cost of the rewards doesn't eat into the donation too much. Don't forget the cost of shipping such items—which can be equal or greater than the cost of printing them. Be sure to seek tax advice before offering tangible rewards.

If your nonprofit offers a membership program, you can utilize that as a reward. Be sure to treat all your members the same, regardless of where you sourced them.

Another common perk used by nonprofits is handicrafts produced by the people you are helping with your program. This works well if you are helping people who are capable of participating in their own relief. Picture a souvenir bracelet made by Cambodian orphans. Your nonprofit may acquire them for $1 and you may be able to "sell" them for $20 or more, allowing you to return even more to the children.

For-profit social ventures don't have any worries about tax implications for perks and rewards, giving you much more room to be creative. You might think of social ventures as falling across a spectrum, from those with social missions as integrated into the business as most nonprofits to for-profit consumer businesses with a cause attached. The more fully integrated the cause, the more the approach you might use a nonprofit's approach. On the other end of the spectrum, however, you may be focusing on your products or services as a reward as much or more than you are focusing on your mission.

Perks that you may want to consider for your social venture would obviously include your product or service if it can be sold on the web—even if it can't be delivered on the web. People will donate—though it may be more modestly—to for-profit social ventures even without a reward.

Consider this example of a product-focused, crowdfunding campaign with a social agenda: Fam Mirza, founder of the 1:Face Watch, raised over $60,000 selling simple watches for $40 via crowdfunding. The watches came in six colors. Each color was matched up to a cause. Fam committed to provide a measurable amount of support to the cause that corresponded to the watch color that supporters chose. (My red watch provided money for AIDS research.)

Be creative in your approach. If your goal is to help people become more environmentally friendly, for instance, consider rewards that would fit. You may be able to get an author to donate digital copies of a book on being green to give away as a perk. This may cost you nothing, but have real value to your supporters. Similarly, you may be able to get perks like that from musicians who believe in what you're doing. You may also be able to provide a personal environmental audit—essentially an interview over the phone—helping people to identify the opportunities in their daily lives to reduce their environmental footprint.

So tap your network, get creative, and find ways to inspire your fans to become backers.

CHAPTER 8

SAM'S BIRTHMARK

Barron Griffin was born a healthy baby boy with a port-wine stain on his face. His parents, Martha and Grant Griffin, decided to write a book called *Sam's Birthmark.* They hoped to start a movement encouraging acceptance of people who have special characteristics that "make them shine as an individual," says Martha Griffin.[7]

The Vascular Birthmarks Association website describes the condition:

"Port-wine stain (PWS) (bit.ly/17t3ICW), also called nevus flammeus, is a congenital, cutaneous vascular malformation involving post-capillary venules which produce a light pink to red- to dark red-violet discoloration of human skin. PWS occurs in an estimated 3 children per 1,000 live births, affecting males and females and all racial groups equally. There appears to be no hereditary predilection for PWS within families. There are no known risk factors or ways to prevent PWS."

7 Most of the information for this article was obtained directly from Martha Griffin via an online interview.

In order to cover the cost of the illustrator, and printing the full-color, beautifully illustrated hard-cover books, they ran a campaign on Kickstarter (kck.st/QAikJc) where they successfully raised $31,763. As rewards for their supporters they offered copies of the book, either as a PDF—or, for the larger donors—the final, hard-bound form. Large donors received special rewards, including signed copies of the book, invitations to the launch party, and acknowledgements in the book.

They raised enough to print 4,000 copies—1,000 more than their original goal.

In order to be successful, Martha says, "We sent numerous e-mail campaigns to our friends, family, and our entire network. We also heavily targeted friends of friends and the Vascular Birthmark community through Facebook."

Martha notes that "the video was key," adding "Mindful Media Productions did a great job."

Using crowdfunding enabled the Griffins to answer four questions:

1. Would the birthmark community embrace or see a need for the book?
2. Would the message appeal to our network and outside the birthmark community?
3. Could we 'market' the book through a viral campaign like Kickstarter?
4. What would be the response to our story?

The successful campaign yielded affirmative answers on all fronts. "The people who pre-bought are people we don't know," Martha told her local paper, *Park Cities People*. "It took off from Kickstarter. It never would have gone viral without it."[8]

Now that the book is published, their Facebook page (on.fb.me/1c1DWxi) is filling up with images of children with birthmarks—including one named Sam—proudly holding a copy of the book. One child posted on the page is from Iceland, suggesting the global potential of their movement.

The Griffins don't plan to stop with just one book. They plan to write a series of books around the theme "What Makes Me Shine." Today, the book is available for sale from www.samsbirthmark.com (bit.ly/13zfCh3). As they said on their Kickstarter page, "He [Barron] inspired us to write for children about how every child in the world is unique and special in their own way.[9]"

8 http://bit.ly/10q4jWx

9 http://arizonafamilies.blogspot.com/2012/10/help-help-publish-book-and-get-copy.html (bit.ly/14XQ0WO)

CHAPTER 9

START BEFORE YOU START

The most surprising thing about crowdfunding is the sheer amount of work you don't see from outside. The work involved is like an iceberg: 10 percent you see, 90 percent is completely out of sight.

If you are serious about raising tens of thousands of dollars with a crowdfunding campaign for your cause, you'll want to start at least four to six weeks before officially launching your campaign.

ORGANIZE YOUR TEAM

Your first order of business is to organize your team. One of the things that successful crowdfunding campaigns have in common is a team of people involved in the planning and execution of the campaign. While bootstrapping a campaign with virtually no money is common, working alone to raise big dollars is somewhere between black swans and unicorns in rarity.

There are lots of ways to organize your team and I won't pretend to tell you exactly how it must be done, but would suggest that there are three basic tiers of people who will help you. You'll want to think about into which group each person on your team fits.

Partners: Your partners are those who will be with you, shoulder to shoulder from start to finish. If you work in a nonprofit organization with other employees, some of the other employees will be your partners in this project—perhaps all of them. Some of your board members will be as well. If you are launching a new social venture, you may have literal financial partners who can help you. Your spouse may also be a good partner. The key definition of a partner is someone you trust with knowing every aspect of your campaign and strategy. You'll likely want to have one partner for every $5,000 you hope to raise.

Champions: Your champions are people who are close enough to you and passionate enough about your project that you can ask them to volunteer time to help you with your campaign. You likely can't direct the work of champions like you might direct the work of some of your partners, but they have the potential to make a huge difference in your campaign. Your champions will likely participate in some planning meetings and will take some assignments to promote your work, but are generally people who will not be working on this as much as you. You should hope to find two or three champions for each partner on the team.

Boosters: Boosters are volunteers who show up to help you make something happen without being asked. Generally, volunteers in a crowdfunding campaign appear out of nowhere after you launch. They will often be as effective as your champions even though they have not been involved in the planning. Likely, they are people who are passionate about what you're doing, but not necessarily in your inner circle (otherwise they'd likely have been tagged as champions). It could include 13-year-old girls who have big social networks and lots of passion or middle-aged executives who have lots of influence and money but little time. While you won't organize them before you launch the campaign, you want to plan for them to join your team. Be prepared to incorporate them into your communications strategy and your fundraising incentives.

Competition: Optimally, you'll choose a platform that allows you to track your fundraisers. Your champions and boosters and even partners may want to track their individual performance. If the platform you choose won't do that, you miss out on a powerful dynamic: competition. Your champions and boosters will want to compete to see who can raise the most money. While some will get discouraged and won't do much (be prepared for that), some will go far beyond the average and beyond your goals and expectations. You should look for creative ways to motivate them to compete for achievements.

Depending on your budget and circumstances, your champions and boosters may compete for pride, for the right to wear a tiara in the office, or for a trip to London. You decide based on all the factors that influence such a thing (including whether or not it would be embarrassing to your cause for someone to get an extravagant prize).

Once you have assembled your team and planned your competition and incentives, you are ready to start preparing to launch.

The success of your campaign may come down to the progress you achieve during the first few hours of the campaign. You don't want anyone outside of your inner circle to arrive at your campaign page and discover that you have raised less than 25 percent of your goal. That presents a challenge, perhaps the biggest challenge of your campaign.

Each of your partners—and you—should plan to reach out to your network on a personal basis. As a guideline, let me suggest the following goals:

- **Five big hitters:** Each of you should identify five big hitters who can easily provide a $500 or $1000 check for your campaign. Schedule a meeting with them to explain why you'd like them to support your campaign and why it is important for them to do it on the first day—even the first hours of the campaign. Your goal with each big hitter is to leave with a firm commitment regarding a dollar amount and the timing of the donation.

- **Fifteen base hitters:** Each of the partners should identify 15 to 30 people who are not big hitters, but who are most likely to make a commitment—however modest—to your campaign. These are your base hitters. Call each of these people and ask them to commit to making their donations as soon as your campaign launches.

- **Thirty to 100 swingers:** Next, you'll want to identify the rest of your friends, fans, followers, and supporters who could be asked directly to give. To each of these the partners will want to send personalized emails explaining the cause, the campaign, and asking for support on day one.

Be sure to create a follow-up communication plan for everyone who agrees to participate. The last thing you want is to lose a donation simply because you didn't stay in touch between getting the commitment and arriving at the start of the campaign.

Implementing this strategy well may allow you to raise half of your money before the campaign even starts. That's the idea. Opinions vary from 10 percent to 70 percent, but on the principle everyone in the crowdfunding community is in agreement. You must get some cash in the tip jar or no one else will contribute. Have at least 25 percent committed before you start and shoot for 50 percent if you can get there.

The very worst thing that could happen if you raise too much money before the campaign starts is that you get a bunch of money on the first day and nothing later. That doesn't sound like the end of the world. If you don't raise any money in advance, the worst thing that could happen is that you never do. Sadly, many campaigns fail to reach their goals largely because they never really got started.

You can set the tone for your entire experience by being over-prepared for the first day of your campaign. If you have half of your goal on the first day, others will feel motivated and excited by your success and you are almost certain to reach and surpass your goal.

One of the keys to a successful campaign is the careful bridging of the real world and the online world. Rarely are campaigns successful if they rely entirely on Facebook and Twitter. Similarly, if you and your partners have small networks online, you're likely to struggle.

In order to bring those two worlds together, have a launch party in various locations connected via Google+ Hangouts so you can see each other and interact. You may even want to broadcast the party.

Broadcasting your party like this creates that perfect connection between your real and online friends. Hosting a Google+ Hangout and broadcasting it openly to everyone in the world is free, too.

Each partner can host a party at his or her own home. Some of your champions may also want to host parties. If you can involve people in various cities or even various countries, you can create even more excitement.

Take time at the party to do several key things. Make sure you spend time talking about the cause, why it matters, and how your campaign's success matters to the cause. You may want to announce the competition among your champions and boosters—if there is a way for more people to sign up as boosters at this point. You'll certainly want to talk about any rewards you are offering to your supporters so they understand not only what's in it for the cause, but what's in it for them.

Above all, it is important to make your launch party fun. Be creative. You don't have to spend a lot of money. You shouldn't spend a lot of money. It can cause others to believe you don't need financial help if you are blowing lots of money on the party.

Once you have your party, the talking is done and the campaign has begun!

CHAPTER 10

TOHL FOUNDERS CROWDFUND THEIR SOCIAL VENTURE

After the earthquake in Haiti in 2010, Aporva Sinha and Benjamin Cohen saw a BBC broadcast of Bill Clinton talking about how there was plenty of water available in the port but that it could not be delivered to people in the city of Port-au-Prince. "People were dying from lack of water even though the water was nearby," Benjamin emphasized.[10]

Benjamin Cohen

The two were deeply troubled by the situation. When another major earthquake struck Chile, it confirmed their desire to solve this problem. Together, they envisioned a sys-

10 Most of the information for this article was obtained directly from Benjamin Cohen through an online interview.

tem that would allow for delivering functioning pipelines in mere hours following a disaster. They launched TOHL later that year.

In the spring of 2012, the founders received $40,000 of seed capital from Start-up Chile and began working to launch the business in earnest. Having designed the system, they were ready to build it and test it. The test went flawlessly and the team was able to deploy a functioning water line over a one-kilometer distance using a helicopter in just nine minutes.

As every entrepreneur knows, such milestones use cash rather than generate it. So, in August, the nascent company launched a crowdfunding campaign on Kickstarter (kck.st/U8Y98a).

Benjamin said, "TOHL executed an exhaustive campaign that included the targeting of personal networks of our team (friends and family), social network penetration (Facebook, Twitter, LinkedIn), targeting of the entrepreneurial community that we are apart of (Start-Up Chile, Singularity University, Georgia Tech, Village Capital)."

He also explained that they made a focused effort to distribute press releases to key people in the media. He said, "We had over 30 articles written about us in a matter of just a few weeks during our campaign in places like Forbes, BBC, Huffington Post, Tree Hugger, Inc., Gizmag, Indian Economic Times, Calgary Herald, and many others."

"We made a last minute push at the very end of the campaign, and found some good friends who helped us close the gap," Benjamin added.

TOHL produced an unusually long, but compelling video for their Kickstarter campaign. Benjamin noted, "The key to crowdfunding is a having a video that clearly and curiously portrays the project that you are working on."

As you review the TOHL campaign on Kickstarter, you'll note that all of the rewards (except the reward for donating $1) involve hard costs. Benjamin explained their strategy, saying, "It also helps to provide backers with good incentives to support. The rewards must make the backers get connected to the project and the rewards also have to have a reasonable level of value, so that the backers feel that they are getting something for the money."

Benjamin counts the Kickstarter campaign a success, despite not generating much cash for their project after covering all of their expenses out of the $30,000 they raised. "The money TOHL raised covered the costs of the video production, the costs of the rewards provided to backers, the fees, the taxes, and the advertising expenses associated with the project. We did not have too much money left over to do the project, but we are seeing the project pay dividends in many other ways. The legitimacy that our Kickstarter campaign created for TOHL is bigger than any money that could have been received. It became a launching point for our venture to some degree," Benjamin said.

The big 2012 project that the campaign helped (a little) to fund was the design and construction of a second spooling mechanism that would be lighter and more versatile than their original design.

TOHL is up and running now. Benjamin describes their business this way: "TOHL delivers water to people who need it urgently. For example, TOHL quickly and cheaply provides a continuous flow of water to natural disaster victims and refugees in camps. In times of drought, when water is out of reach, TOHL helps farmers save their crops. TOHL also limits the damage caused by forest fires. We deliver water more rapidly, more reliably, and closer to the flames than other solutions to help extinguish the fire faster. TOHL's social benefits are clear: we save lives, preserve livelihoods, protect homes, and conserve resources."

Benjamin adds, "TOHL created an installation method that combines the use of long segments of piping that are deployed by helicopter in order to be able to complete pipeline installations in remote locations quickly, more directly, and in a less environmentally destructive way. TOHL wins contracts because competitors are slower, more expensive, and more environmentally damaging."

Benjamin notes that TOHL operates today with a triple-bottom-line approach, seeking to help people, protect the planet, and generate a profit.

CHAPTER 11

PRODUCING A VIRAL VIDEO FOR YOUR CAMPAIGN

Everyone wants to create a truly viral video for their campaign. The reality is that if we really knew exactly what it took to create a video that would garner a million views or more, all videos would get that many views because people would only make videos like that. The fact is it requires a measure of luck.

What we can do is explain how to create a video that will enhance your message—rather than hurt it—allowing you to maximize the potential of your campaign.

One thing to keep in mind is that while campaigns with videos significantly outperform campaigns without videos, the ones that have videos are likely to have a variety of other things going for them as well. In other words, your video is important but it may not be of make-or-break importance to the campaign. It is, however, the single most important element of what you put on your campaign page, so take it seriously.

Face: You want your video to introduce people to the face of your campaign. If your cause will raise money for starving children, you'll want starving children—in fact a single starving child—to be the face of your campaign. If you are raising money for an animal shelter, use video with a particularly cute animal from the shelter. Do your best to find a person or animal to use as the traditional poster child for your campaign.

You: Next, you need to connect yourself (presuming you are the leader of the organization) to the campaign. While you may not be the reason or purpose for the campaign, you need to use the video to connect you and your organization to the cause by placing yourself in the video with the poster child or face of your campaign.

Authenticity: Your primary goal is build a relationship of trust with people in the short length of your video. Again, this requires that you actually appear in the video, that you speak to the audience, and look into the camera to connect with your audience. Your goal is to connect with people, to let them feel your passion for the cause, and to establish credibility.

Brevity: Your video should be shorter than three minutes. Some people won't even click to watch a video that is longer than three minutes, so having a video that is two minutes and 59 seconds long is better than one that is three minutes and one second. That said, some campaigns have been successful at raising tens of thousands of dollars with much longer videos. There is no minimum length for your video. If you can convey your entire message in thirty seconds, do it.

Attention: Once you get someone to click your video you want to be sure to capture their attention in the first 30 seconds of the video. If it is boring, you'll lose people. Be sure to summarize as much information about the campaign in the first 30 seconds. That way, those who don't watch the full video at least understand your cause and can make a vaguely informed decision about whether or not to contribute to your campaign.

Use the Power of the Medium: A video is a powerful tool for sharing images, sound and action. Don't make the mistake of creating a five-minute video of a talking head (yours or anyone else's) rambling on about the cause. Regardless of the passion, you'll be losing out on the potential of the tool. By sharing images of the people you'll help, the problems that exist, the changes you'll make—or at least that you plan to make—will make your campaign real. You can accomplish much of this objective inexpensively with still images integrated into the video.

Tell a Story: A story doesn't just have a beginning, a middle, and an end. It has a context, a crisis, and a resolution. You need to set the stage, present the hope for the resolution, and explain the challenges that threaten the world you seek to create. Make your audience feel as if you and they working together can overcome the crisis to bring about the hoped-for change in the world.

The Ask: With all else that you are doing in your video, don't forget to ask for what you want. Be specific with what you'd like. If you really hope to get $100 from every person, ask for it. Tell them why you need it, what you'll do with it, and what they'll get for it. Also, sharing your campaign is worth money. Always, always, always ask people to share the campaign with their friends via email, Facebook, Twitter or other social media even if they can't support you financially.

The Five Ws: Don't forget to include all the basics in your video: who, what, where, when, and why. Review your script carefully to ensure that these details are included. Don't leave people wondering who you are or who you are helping. Don't let them wonder what you are doing, where you are doing it, or how you are doing it for that matter. You can create a proper sense of urgency by including specific dates in your campaign that will cause people to donate and share now rather than leave them thinking they can come back to this another time.

Video tips: Unless you are planning a six-figure campaign and have substantial resources in terms of staff, advertising, promotion and a huge network, you should probably plan to create your video yourself or with the help of a friend or volunteer with a camera and a basic laptop. The camera itself is remarkably unimportant. Your phone may do an adequate job. The key to good video is good lighting. Avoid shooting outside in windy conditions as the wind may create background noise that competes violently with spoken audio. If you can shoot with a camera connected wirelessly to a microphone, your audio track will sound much better. If not, shoot inside with great lighting in quiet places and your video will look and sound good enough.

Tools and Resources: There are a lot of free and cheap resources available to help you build a video for your campaign if you have a mind to do it yourself.

- **Movie Maker or iMovie:** Most computers come with either Movie Maker (for Windows) or iMovie (for the Mac). These programs allow you to edit your video with virtually no training. If you'd like a quick how-to, you can find handy videos that explain how to use these tools on YouTube for free.
- **Music:** Your video can be enhanced meaningfully by some music. YouTube won't let you upload music you don't own the rights to use so you can't just use music you bought for your iPhone. There a variety of web sites that sell single tracks that you can use as background music for your video, including RoyaltyFreeMusic.com (bit.ly/ihME3d) and PremiumBeat.com (bit.ly/fLl1vF) (you guessed it—the latter site is more expensive).
- **Sparkol:** At Sparkol.com you can download software that will help you make a video where a hand draws a message on a whiteboard. After you create the video there, you'll need to add audio.
- **Animoto:** With Animoto.com you can upload a collage of photos and have them matched to royalty-free music in a professional and appealing way. You still need to add a narrative track to such a video and you have to pay to download a high-definition version of the file, but it is a relatively simple way to create a beautiful looking video from a collection of still images. This may be helpful if you have stills but can't afford to return to the location where you'd like to shoot the video—for example, if your cause is to help a village in Kenya and you have great photos from your last visit but no video.
- **Picasa:** At Picasa.com (bit.ly/cdcG0r) by Google you can download free software for your computer that will take a collection of photos and string them together in a video. You can then add music using Movie Maker or iMovie.

Before making your video, go watch some campaign videos. In fact, make a point to watch ten and rank them in order from best to worst, based on the criteria discussed in this chapter. Pay special attention to any that make you want to donate or share.

As one of your ten, watch the campaign video for CleanBirth.org here: youtu.be/UD2Zw-lfwgw. The campaign video isn't perfect, but it includes an effective use of many of the criteria in this chapter. When I watched the video—just looking for a good example video to share—and I saw this one I both donated to the cause and shared the video.

Whether you work alone or with a friend who has more videography experience, you can create a video that will tell your story and move people to action without breaking the bank.

CHAPTER 12

KADEN

When Kaden Benoit was born in December 2011, following a stressful delivery, he was rushed to the neonatal intensive care unit because he was not breathing on his own.[11]

Before leaving the hospital, he was diagnosed with hearing loss. But that was just the tip of the iceberg. As months progressed, Kaden failed to develop normally, not lifting his head, not learning to crawl, or moving around at the point when babies normally reach those milestones.

His pediatrician once suggested that he might have a metabolic disorder, which—upon doing some internet research—sent his parents into a panic. That same day, they took Kaden to the emergency room at The Hospital for Sick Children universally known as SickKids Hospital in Toronto near their home. He was admitted and seen by a panel of specialists.

Ultimately, he was diagnosed with an extremely rare condition—there are only about 20 documented cases in

11 Much of the information for this story was provided directly by Aida Kadic through an online interview.

the world. He has a genetic deletion and is missing 37 genes. Doctors only have a clear idea what just one of those genes do, so understanding Kaden's future is challenging.

But some things are clear, however. He has central hypotonia or low-muscle tone, global developmental delays, and is at risk for epileptic seizures and other unknown risks. He also has auditory neuropathy spectrum disorder, which causes profound deafness and can't be treated with a cochlear implant. He is a candidate for an experimental spinal implant that is available only in Italy.

Kaden is also far-sighted and requires glasses, which will need to be replaced regularly as he grows. He also uses hearing aids that require new ear molds on a regular basis.

Kaden needs daily physical and occupational therapy that falls outside the scope of covered treatments under the Ontario Health Insurance Plan (OHIP). These sessions would cost the family $300 per day.

Facing all of this, Kaden's parents Aida Kadic and Len Benoit took the advice and counsel of friends; they set up a crowdfunding campaign on Indiegogo (bit.ly/1cDfNv4) to raise the money they needed to properly care for their son, giving him a chance to learn to develop normally. "[I] want him to learn to sit, stand, walk, run and talk... desperately," Aida said.

Aida and Len made their video at home. She describes it as the biggest challenge they faced in running the campaign. The lengthy 11-minute video is a photo slideshow of Kaden from birth forward, interspersed with text that tells Kaden's tragic story. She said it "took us a few days" to compile the video.

Given the nature of the campaign, the Kadics offered no rewards. Of course, no one complained. People were eager to help. In fact, Aida noted that one of the challenges of the campaign was "keeping up with all the people wanting to help and wanting to know more."

Aida's own social network was small, but she reached out to all of her friends and famiy for help and pushed her 200 Facebook friends to share Kaden's story. One of their big challenges was getting and keeping people's attention. The best tool they had was their Facebook page.

Their big break came when a local television station did a story (bit.ly/1b6MQG0) about Kaden. "This helped our skeptics know that this is for real and we really needed help for our son," Aida said.

The two-minute story captured the hearts of the people in their community. By the end of their campaign, they had raised $32,203 from 178 people. One person (or perhaps two people with the same name), Murat Mujcinovic, donated $3,900. Many donations show up on the roster as "undisclosed" amounts, but among those that are public, a majority gave over $100. They also raised another $22,000 at a silent auction; Aida credits that to their online efforts as well.

Kaden's Facebook page (on.fb.me/1b6Ne7n) is now replete with photos of his physical therapy and the progress he's making, even sitting up to watch television. Aida says, "He is doing awesome!" As a result of therapy, Kaden can now drink from a bottle all by himself. He also plays with his toys, babbles and—Aida hopes—will learn to speak. She says his performance is so remarkable that doctors recently sought a release to publish reports about his progress; she eagerly complied.

He has a long road ahead of him and the money raised in 2012 won't last forever, but he's off to a good start.

Aida notes, "I have been learning so much about life and feel at ease knowing that the world is a better place than I ever thought was possible. There is a lot more good in the world than bad."

CHAPTER 13

LEVERAGING YOUR NETWORK

Everyone who understands anything about crowdfunding appreciates that "your network" is somehow key to the success of the campaign. Most, however, don't appreciate how this really works. Getting your network to donate to and share your campaign will take work. Lots of work.

If you have even a modicum of passion for your cause, this should be the fun part of your campaign—the part you've been looking forward to doing. This is where you tell your story to your friends and followers, conveying your enthusiasm and the substance of what you're doing and why.

A typical crowdfunding campaign will last 30 to 60 days; 45 days is pretty common. Some last as little as one day and others last for months (often extended because of their success).

As we've discussed previously, you'll want to plan to connect with your network regularly. You'll want to be sure to post on Facebook, Twitter, Google+ and LinkedIn—plus any other social networks where you already have a following on a regular basis. Every social networking platform has its own rhythm, rules and culture. In order to leverage each to its full potential, consider the following suggestions:

EBOOK

Facebook is the unquestioned king of social networking as I write this. If you are going to have a successful crowdfunding campaign you must think about how you'll leverage Facebook. If you don't have a lot of Facebook friends today, start working on that. Even if you are not naturally a social butterfly, you need to get on Facebook and start "friending" everyone you know.

Many people have reasonable thoughts of using Facebook as a tool for maintaining relationships with actual friends; others use it as a way to meet new people. If you want to be successful with crowdfunding, you should think about Facebook as a way to maintain contact with everyone you've ever known. The vast majority of them are already on Facebook; you just need to find them. Facebook, like most other social networking programs, will allow you to connect your email list to Facebook to identify all of the people you know there and automatically extend a friend request. Do this. It will save you time and help you connect with a crowd in a hurry.

Once you have your network on Facebook, here are some tips for building relationships there. Stay away from politics (unless your cause is, strictly speaking, political). Don't give people a reason to unfriend you or ignore you. Be generous with "likes." If a friend posts something that is not objectionable, "like" it as a way of casually interacting. Comment—always supportively—on interesting posts your friends make. Never has the axiom your mother offered you as a child been more important: if you don't have something nice to say, don't say anything at all. Let your friends political screeds go unanswered; let some other self-declared judge of truth or grammar fight the battles—you're out to build a following.

On Facebook, it is readily acceptable for you to post several times each day. It is less appreciated by your friends if you post six things right in a row. Six things two hours apart is generally viewed more favorably. You can use BufferApp.com to schedule your posts across many platforms throughout the day to avoid clogging up your friends' feeds with lumps of posts from you.

During your campaign, be sure to post about all the things you normally do. Share a personal anecdote, a cute cat picture, a funny video, a snapshot of your dinner or whatever else you'd like to share. A wide variety of posts are acceptable on Facebook; you'll be more interesting to more people if you have a wider range of things to say.

Be sure to post about your campaign at least once and perhaps twice every day during the run of the campaign. You can update people on your progress, talk about what you'll be doing with the money and you can't thank people too much for their support. Be sure to thank everyone you know who contributes on Facebook.

TWITTER

Twitter is used by barely more than 10 percent of people on Facebook, though it is continuing to grow rapidly. The Twitter community is generally a bit less personal and much more public. Most people make their posts available publicly—not just to their friends—so the dialogue there tends to reflect that, with somewhat less introspection and personal interaction.

The 160-character limit of a tweet also tends to discourage personal dialogue. The limit forces a level of verbal efficiency that is sometimes frustrating to write, but can be refreshing to read. The challenge when writing a tweet is to say something truly interesting in the space allotted.

Relationship building on Twitter is somewhat different than elsewhere. While there is a private, direct message feature on Twitter, it is seldom used but by spammers. To actually reach people, you generally want to tweet them using their Twitter @handle; this is called a "mention." Most regular users of Twitter check their "interactions" regularly, allowing them to see who is engaging with them in one way or another. Beware that if you mention someone who isn't following you, they may mark your tweet as spam and your account could be suspended. You'll want to be sure to primarily mention only your friends and followers to avoid that problem.

One common and respectful way of getting attention from someone you'd like to follow you is to "retweet" their posts from time to time. Don't do it indiscriminately, but when someone else tweets something your followers would find interesting, retweeting is a simple and easy way to deliver a compliment to the person who posted it with the potential result of picking up a follow.

Note, too, that there is a limit to the number of tweets, retweets, follows and other actions that you are allowed each day. Be patient. If you aren't on Twitter before your campaign starts, chances are it won't help you much with this campaign to start now. Remember this: you will almost certainly do another crowdfunding campaign again. Use your first campaign to learn the ropes and build your network for a much more successful second campaign.

Most tweets, or at least a large minority, include a link to something else. You'll almost always want to include a link to your campaign page when you tweet an update. The trick is to entice your followers—and others who may happen upon your tweet—to click the link to visit your campaign page. Don't be boring.

GOOGLE+

As I write this, Google+ does not seem to be a particularly important tool for sharing your campaign, but I believe that appearances are wrong. Because Google decides what people find, it makes sense to put some of your content on Google+ where Google is likely to find it—helping others to discover it.

More importantly, I believe that the Google Hangout application is the "killer app" for communicating your message publicly. You can do a Hangout with up to ten people scattered around the world and then make that Hangout public with one click. You can post the video feed anywhere, just like you'd post a YouTube video (the Hangout will also automatically be live on YouTube and on your Google+ profile page).

Think about that tool for a moment. You can be your own CNN. You can interview people, broadcast it live, and archive the video for all to see. It is an amazing technology. Even if you don't use this technology, other people will. As a result, Google+ will become increasingly relevant over time. Don't be stubborn; engage on Google+.

STRATEGY

As you post on all of these platforms each day, it will be tempting—if only because it is so much work—to post once or twice per day about your campaign and leave it at that. If you do, you'll become like a one-note symphony and your friends will tune you out. You'll want to continue engaging with your friends in the same way you did before—or should have been—by posting personal things, jokes, photos and all the rest.

Make a point to spend time reading what your friends are posting on each platform, interact with them and demonstrate true friendship; demonstrate your interest in others. You are likely to do this naturally. But even other-oriented people like you, who live your lives to serve and help others, sometimes get so focused on a specific group of others (abused women, starving children, homeless families, etc.) that they forget to apply some of their concern for others toward their friends and followers on social media. Save some compassion for your network.

STATUS UPDATES

On all of your platforms you'll want to update people on progress toward your goals regularly. Be sure to celebrate key milestones along the way. Report on your progress specifically at least once per week.

When you update friends on your progress, remember three things: progress toward the goal, gratitude, and your purpose:

Progress: Your friends and followers will be interested to know how you are doing. Those who have already supported you, as well as your other friends, will be inspired by the progress you are making. Put the numbers out there. Be proud of what you've done, even if you need to acknowledge that you need more help because you aren't on track for reaching your goal. Be honest and optimistic in your progress updates.

Gratitude: Don't ever update your progress without an expression of thanks to all who have supported you so far. Regularly thank your supporters individually on Facebook and Twitter so that they feel recognized for their donations. In addition, when you post a progress update, be sure to add an expression of appreciation to all of your contributors.

Purpose: Do your best to remind people in every progress post of your purpose. Remind them that the money you raise helps you accomplish your social mission. If you can, put your progress in terms of the good you'll do, as in, "Thank you for helping us provide clean water for 500 people with your donations, now totaling $5,000!" In that simple sentence, you'll have hit all three of the update points: progress, gratitude, and purpose.

In every single post about your campaign, be sure to include the link to the page where you are accepting donations. You'd hate to get someone's attention and then not give them a way to find and help you easily. We all have short attention spans, especially on the web where everything is one big distraction. If you force a follower to do a Google search, they'll be watching cat videos and your contribution will be long forgotten in about 23 seconds.

Plan to dedicate time regularly throughout the day to post updates across all of your social media platforms—not just Facebook, Twitter and Google+. Be sure you are connecting with everyone you can. You can build an audience. You can raise money for your cause. You can change the world. Your friends, fans, and followers want to help. Let them!

CHAPTER 14

THE RAINBOW SUMMITS

Cason Crane has already summited all seven of the tallest peaks on the planet, known as the Seven Summits. Considered an incredible achievement for any mountaineer, at age 19, Cason became one of the youngest ever to accomplish the feat. More importantly, he became the first openly gay person ever to do it.[12]

Cason Crane, after summiting Everest

Cason turned to crowdfunding to add meaning to his mission. He doesn't need the money to pay for his mountaineering. He's raising money for the Trevor Project, the organization responsible for the "It Gets Better" cam-

12 Most of the information for this story was provided directly by Cason Crane via an online interview.

paign fighting LBGTQ teen suicide. Every dollar raised goes straight to the Trevor Project—he never touches the money.

Cason was inspired to make this his campaign when his friend Charlotte killed herself while they were in high school. His passion and commitment to the cause was steeled when Tyler Clementi committed suicide after his roommate Dharun Ravi and a friend, Molly Wei, surreptitiously broadcast live images of Tyler kissing another man. As a gay man of the same age living in the same state, Cason felt connected to Clementi despite not knowing him personally.

Cason said, "I knew that I needed to make a difference on this issue so that in the future no youth, LGBTQ or otherwise, considered or attempted suicide."

Cason has now summited all seven (actually eight peaks because there is some disagreement among climbers about the highest peak in or around Australia). Cason was actually on Everest as I was writing the first draft of this chapter!

"My biggest challenge," he said, "was definitely learning how to ask people for money. Even though my cause is 100% charitable and I don't get anything out of it, I still felt guilty, nervous, and embarrassed making 'the ask.' This is when I turned to social media and crowdfunding. It allowed me to focus less on getting big, high-dollar contributions and more on spreading my message (and raising more awareness!) and encouraging people to make smaller donations, or gather a group of their friends to each make a small donation. This strategy allowed me to raise tens of thousands of dollars."

He created a video with the help of a friend of his father who volunteered to produce the video, a short film that includes a brief interview with Cason and footage of him mountaineering. The video, which he did not place on his Razoo (bit.ly/13TrSnP) campaign page, has been viewed more than 5,000 times. "I don't think that the video, in the end, did very much to further my cause because it didn't ever move beyond my existing circle of friends and supporters. (It didn't "go viral.") That said, it obviously did not hurt my cause," he explained.

In order to raise money, Cason has been taking opportunities—between climbs—to speak to audiences about his work. He says, "I had to overcome a fear of public speaking so that I could effectively spread awareness and bring my story and mission to other kids and communities around the country."

Of course, the greatest challenge has been actually climbing the Seven Summits, a challenge he describes as "formidable."

In order to create a successful campaign—at this point his campaign has raised over $100,000 toward his goal of $250,000—he "focused at first on just building a network on social media." He created a website (bit.ly/Z7hUPe), including a blog, and a Facebook page (on.fb.me/16oQzvD) that now has over 10,000 "likes." Even before he started, he says he had "several thousand" Facebook friends as well as several hundred on Twitter (bit.ly/13MG8VN) (he now has over 1,800 followers).

After starting with his existing base, Cason wanted to build his social network quickly. "I then used the Facebook Advertising service to get more followers that way, which was very successful. I used the Twitter Ad service to get more followers on my Twitter account as well," he said. He's spent $2,000 to date promoting his campaign.

"Simultaneously, I reached out to press and media and sought attention that way, which were great for getting more followers and contributions through my online pages," he added.

No matter what happens from here, Cason has been a huge success. He's significantly increased awareness of his cause, making it easier for teens to come out and avoid suicide. He's raised over $100,000 for his cause and has, along the way, climbed some of the highest peaks on Earth.

Cason was successful with his climbing and has raised over $135,000 for the Trevor Project. While climbing was largely up to Cason, the achievement of his goal to raise $250,000 may be up to you.

CHAPTER 15

EXPAND YOUR REACH WITH BLOGS AND TRADITIONAL MEDIA

Blogs and traditional media have the potential to radically expand your reach. Based on my personal research talking to successful cause-oriented crowdfunders, the key to a big win is traditional media. For all the potential of social media—which truly is the core of crowdfunding—getting your message in the local paper, on the radio, or television has the potential to amplify your message and attract multiples of the money you and your team can raise from your network alone. Here is a plan to help you.

Many bloggers and the traditional media like to write about heart-warming, human interest stories. That said, they neither have the time nor the ability to hunt down your story. You have to find them and feed it to them.

START WITH YOUR FRIENDS; BUILD FROM THERE

Everyone knows a few bloggers. Make a list of every blogger you know, regardless of what they blog about. Focus this list on people you actually know, people who may write about what you're doing as a favor because they know you.

Next, identify bloggers who write about topics related to your cause. You can do a search on Google for phrases related specifically to your cause. If you are raising money to combat hunger in your community, you might search for blogs about your community or blogs about hunger, but what you really want to find are blogs about hunger in your town. Let Google do the hard work.

Visit each blog, identify the author, and find a contact point. If the "contact me" or "about me" tab on the blog doesn't include an email address, try to find a LinkedIn or Google+ profile somewhere that does include an email. If you can't find an email, most bloggers have a Twitter handle that you can use to make contact (with the goal of getting an email address).

PROVIDE THE STORY

People who write blogs, especially those that are well-read, are not likely suffering from a lack of ideas. They get pitched ideas far more often than they have time to write about them. Your first goal, when writing to bloggers, is to capture their attention.

The best way to capture their attention is to give them a genuine compliment about their writing. Demonstrate that you've taken the time to read what they write and help them connect what they've written about in the past to your topic. Think along these lines, "I loved your post about hunger in our community and thought you'd be interested in my project..."

The next thing to remember is how busy bloggers are. Even if they write full-time, remember they are busy, working hard (it is funny how often my friends suggest that, because I am a full-time writer that I'm effectively retired, despite the fact that I've never worked harder in my life). You don't merely want to give bloggers a story idea, you want to give them the story. Send a formal press release that is a short news article they have your permission to print as their own. More about that in a minute.

Lastly, you want to be clear with bloggers that you are available to be interviewed. Increasingly, bloggers are using radio-like podcasts to distribute material and as I've mentioned, video interviews with Google+ are also growing. Let them know you're available for whatever they need to make their story.

Now, let's talk about that press release. There are lots of tools online; use one to help you follow the standard format so that media professionals will recognize it. An adequate tool, as an example, can be found at WikiHow (http://bit.ly/XONPCZ).

Apart from your friends, bloggers and writers in the traditional media will give your email just a split second of review. Literally, you have on the order of three seconds to get their attention. Your headline is critical; it must be factual, tell the story and demand that you read the article. You need to create a huge expectation and then deliver on that expectation in the body of your release, beginning with the first paragraph.

It is almost universal that a good press release will include a quote or two, likely from you. In that context, you can write that you've said anything because you're writing it and saying it as you write it. Be as clever as you can be while staying laser-focused on your cause.

While you want your press release to drive people to your crowdfunding campaign page, don't forget that the simple fact that you are crowdfunding isn't interesting. What is interesting is your cause, your purpose, your story. Focus on that and then drive people to action, to get involved, and to help you by supporting your campaign.

To reach traditional media, you may consider a press release. PR Web offers low cost distribution of press releases, but most traditional media outlets ignore releases from PR Web. PR Newsire is used somewhat more by the media, but distribution there is more expensive. All such outreach efforts have the advantage of putting your news out into the World Wide Web, but my experience with such broadcasts is that they yield little more than sales calls from vendors who are happy to help you spend the money you raise.

A personal contact from you—or a friend on your behalf—to someone in the media is much more likely to be effective.

Your most likely coverage in the media is with your local media. Radio, in my personal experience, is the most powerful medium among television, radio and newspapers. Be sure to reach out to every talk show personality in town who may have an interest in your topic. It may take some time to identify them, but radio shows that are on daily do have a need to find interesting people to have on their shows each day. Make sure they know about you and why you'd make a great guest.

You can identify individuals who may write about your issue by visiting your local paper's website and looking for the staff. As they are in the newsgathering business, they generally have a list of email addresses and phone numbers on the website to help you identify exactly the right person to contact.

Television people are often the most difficult to reach, but most television stations have websites with at least some general email address for sending news tips. Use that if you can't find a better contact to get your message inside the station. You can also try to interact with key reporters through their Twitter accounts, but many ignore Twitter interactions.

Remember, the media loves a good human-interest story. The broadcast media folks have a regulatory obligation to serve their communities, so they are effectively required to air some stories about causes. You can bring attention to your cause and your campaign, and you can reach your fundraising goals. Don't be shy and don't shy away from the work. Before you know it, people all around your community will be talking about you and your cause.

CHAPTER 16

SILICON VALLEY EDUCATION FOUNDATION ROCKS CROWDFUNDING

Like many people in non-profit organizations, Muhammed Chaudhry, President and CEO of the Silicon Valley Education Foundation (bit.ly/4w3FLC) was intrigued by the idea of crowdfunding. In 2012, he decided to take the leap.[13]

Muhammed Chaudhry

Traditionally, the foundation's funding came in the form of large donations from well-heeled supporters, foundations and corporations. Seeking out small donations would repre-

13 Most of the information for this story came from a telephone interview with Muhammed Chaudhry.

sent a totally new approach.

Muhammed says they took it seriously, with planning beginning months in advance. One person on the staff, the head of marketing, was designated as the campaign manager, but all members of the staff were encouraged to be involved. They called their campaign "$30k in 30 days." (bit.ly/13Hwnmn)

Their key area of focus in advance of the formal start to the campaign was to line up "fundraisers." In Fundly (bit.ly/13Hwnmn) parlance, a fundraiser is an individual who sets up her own page to raise money for the cause. (In this book, I've often referred to these folks as "champions" or "boosters.")

The organization spent hours helping to train them on techniques for raising money. Two of the fundraisers were organizations, the Hispanic Foundation and Wells Fargo. Each offered a matching donation and they were extremely successful, together raising about one-third of the total for the organization.

The other 19 fundraisers had varying success. Amy Wong raised $1,900 and Jennifer Li raised $1,480. On the other hand, nine of the 19 individuals who had agreed to raise money for the campaign show as having raised nothing. While they may have recruited donors to the campaign's main page and otherwise helped in the campaign, it is easy to believe that some champions and boosters, when it comes right down to it, can't ask their friends to donate money.

Nonetheless, the fundraisers, including the Hispanic Foundation and Wells Fargo, raised about 60 percent of the money for the campaign (bit.ly/13Hwnmn).

In order to be sure to appeal to the social media generation, they focused on recruiting young people as fundraisers. One high school student who was volunteering in the office explained to Muhammed that he wouldn't post his request at 2:00 in the afternoon while he was in the office because none of his friends would be online at that time. Instead he preferred to post at 8:00 pm when his friends would be online. Muhammed reported that the young man was rather successful in his fundraising efforts.

In addition to the work with its champions and boosters, SVEF also sent mass emails out to its existing supporters. One interesting note from my conversation with Muhammed was that SVEF did not produce or post a video for the campaign. Like most nonprofits, SVEF did not offer any rewards to donors, just a clear explanation of the potential impact of their donations.

Muhammed explained that there were two great challenges for the campaign. The first was recruiting and training the fundraisers. The second challenge was getting the organization on board with the effort. Ultimately, all of the employees participated by sharing the campaign with their own social networks.

The campaign raised over $27,000, nearly reaching the SVEF goal of $30,000. Muhammed characterized the campaign as a big success, noting that while the campaign merely covered its costs, the donor acquisition cost was low. They hope to be able to go back to these 223 donors in the future for more money. Ultimately, they hope to raise another $150,000 as a direct result of the campaign.

Of the lessons learned from the experience, Muhammed notes, "Money won't just come. You have to do the work. The quick and easy doesn't usually work."

SVEF is a nonprofit organization that advocates on behalf of public schools in Silicon Valley, to ensure that these schools have the highest level of post-secondary capability in the country. They focus especially on enhancing the teaching of science, technology, engineering and math. SVEF also provides direct grants to teachers of from $500 to $1,000 for classroom technology that will enhance teaching and learning.

CHAPTER 17

BUILD RELATIONSHIPS OF TRUST

Whatever you are doing with crowdfunding, your first goal should be to build relationships of trust with your supporters. You want them to help spread the word; that requires trust. You want them to back your next campaign; that requires trust. You may want them to volunteer; that requires trust. You need your supporters to trust you, so let's talk about how you do that.

AUTOMATED "THANK-YOU"

Your crowdfunding platform will almost certainly require you to set up an automated thank-you note for your campaign that may also serve as a tax receipt if you are running a nonprofit. Don't settle on the boring, boilerplate template the platform provides; personalize it. Provide your supporters with a genuine, heart-felt thank-you. You may wish to create a thank-you video that all donors receive. As we discussed in Chapter 7, you will also want to create customized thank-you notes and videos that are appropriate to the donor level. For the automated thank-you, which is just the first step, you should customize the form to your organization as much as possible so people really feel that they have been thanked immediately for their support.

UPDATES

Your platform should provide you with an easy way to send updates to your backers. This may be by downloading a contact list or by using a platform-enabled email tool. Whatever the process, be sure to provide weekly updates.

The first key message in your updates should be an expression of genuine appreciation for the money that your supporters have provided, and the promotion they've done on your behalf. Be effusive in your thanks.

Your second message should be an update on the progress of the campaign. If your progress is slow, be sure to admit it. Use that as a trigger for a call to action from your supporters. People want to be a part of a winning team. Help them to feel that they are already part of a big success or that with just a bit more effort on their part they can be.

Your third message element should be to discuss the impact of the campaign's success. Use language like, "with the money we've raised so far we'll be able to accomplish great things." Be as specific as possible. Even if you can't tie money directly to specific activities, use examples. Explain how the money will have an impact on the social cause. If the money is going to help you set up a for-profit business that will in turn support a social cause, be sure to include an update on the impact of the money on the business.

Your final message should be a call to action. As all of the people who will receive this message have already given money, you know they support you and want you to succeed. Give them tools to help share the news. Provide a tweet-length update that they can post to Facebook, Twitter, Google+, LinkedIn, etc. Make it easy for them. Make sure the message is something they'll be proud to post, like, "I'm supporting this great cause that has already raised thousands of dollars to help alleviate suffering." Be sure to tack a short link onto the end of the update.

Using the four key messages in your weekly updates will keep your supporters excited and sharing your message. Note that one of the messages is not to ask for more money. No matter how little someone may have given you, never ask for more. That is the fastest way to lose a supporter. Don't get me wrong; in another six months or a year, you can and should go back to all of your supporters with another campaign. They'll be ready then—just not twice in the same campaign.

AFTER THE CAMPAIGN

After the campaign, depending upon your circumstances, you may have a great deal left to tell your supporters.

Thank-you recognition: Following the campaign, you'll want to be sure to provide the promised recognition as soon as possible. If the promised recognition is connected to another event or product, be sure to update your supporters on the status of the promised acknowledgement periodically. Avoid having to explain why the promised recognition is past due by giving yourself plenty of time up front. If there is a delay, be sure to give yourself plenty of time in your amended promise so that you won't have to back with a third date.

Rewards: If you've promised rewards, keep supporters posted on the status of the rewards. Don't leave folks wondering if you've taken their money and forgotten to deliver the promised goods. If your social cause is a powerful one, your supporters will likely be patient with you, but the key to garnering that patience is honest communication. As with the recognition, don't promise earlier delivery than you can meet. If you're going to miss the delivery date once, do all you can by both working to deliver as soon as possible and by communicating realistic delivery dates so you won't have to explain "another" delay.

Impact: Remember that your supporters will generally have given you money because they want, above all, to see you do some good in the world. The recognition and rewards are just gravy; if you love mashed potatoes and gravy you know how important the gravy is, but it is still just gravy. The meat and potatoes your backers bought is the impact you promised to have. Provide regular updates on your progress toward the promised impact. If there are delays or problems, be upfront. As with recognition and rewards, be sure to give yourself time to execute your plan, especially if you have to go back with an update that acknowledges you are behind schedule. Take the opportunity to provide a new, smarter, and more realistic schedule.

THE NEXT CAMPAIGN

If you've done everything right, most of the people who supported you in your initial campaign will be ready to join you in your second. Keep in mind that you'll always lose some. Don't be overly anxious about losing a few fans or followers along the way. Focus on growing your audience by treating everyone who supports you with trust and support.

You will know you are ready for your next campaign when you have done what you promised to do in the first campaign. If you didn't raise enough in the first campaign to finish what you promised, consider looking for government, corporate, or foundation grants to close the gap so that you don't have to go back to your crowdfund supporters to ask for more help.

A well-executed campaign is like the instructions for shampoo: lather, rinse, repeat. Lathering is the campaign, rinsing is delivering on your promises, and then you're ready to repeat. Every time you repeat you can grow your base of support, your impact, and your mark on the world.

CHAPTER 18

VIVIENNE VOWS TO END CHILD SLAVERY IN HER LIFETIME

In April 2012, Eric Harr and his wife were out for a date and visited the Sonoma Gallery of Lisa Kristine (bit.ly/3uGSbB), a photographer and anti-slavery activist. One of the photos reduced his wife to tears. They bought a book of the art and took it home.[14]

Their then eight-year-old daughter Vivienne recounts what happened in her own words, "I saw a picture (bit.ly/11HMNh2) of two boys with big rocks strapped across their heads. To feel better, they were holding hands. I learned that these boys are brothers ... and slaves. I thought slavery ended with Abraham Lincoln. But it still happens. I wanted to do something about it, because compassion is not compassion without action. It's just feeling sorry for someone."

"We need to help these boys," she told her parents.

14 Most of the information for this story was provided by Eric Harr in a telephone interview.

Vivienne set up a lemonade stand to raise money to end slavery on June 25, 2012. With her parents' help they went to Doc Edgar Park and set up the stand.

Eric says, "People who came were brought to tears that this child was trying to end child slavery." By the end of the day, she earned so much money for the fight that she wanted to do it again. And then again and again.

Vivienne said to her father, "I want to help a lot of these kids. I want to raise a whole $100,000."

Eric realized then that the only way to have the impact Vivienne wanted was to let the world take part.

Vivienne hit upon a new pricing strategy. "Why not let people pay what's in their hearts?" From then on, her lemonade was officially "free because every child should be free." The average amount collected for the lemonade jumped from $2 to $18 per cup. One person paid $1,000, Eric says.

On day 52, Nicholas Kristof, author of *Half the Sky*, tweeted the story.

After Nicholas Kristof tweeted about the lemonade stands, everything began to change. Eric recognized that that this would potentially put Vivienne in a challenging place with increasing media attention.

On day #173, Vivienne reached her goal and wrote a check to Not For Sale for $101,320. When her parents said: "You did it, honey! You're done!" Vivienne said: "Is child slavery done?" Her parents shook their heads. "Then, I am not done," she said.

He asked her if she would rather quit or "find her voice" to share the message broadly through the media. She told him, "I want to find my voice." Vivienne went all the way to day #365, at which point she announced the production of her "bottles of hope" that moved her from street corners to grocery aisles!

Since then, Eric has trusted Vivienne to define her own limits and make her own decisions. Above all, he's completely set aside tactics and strategies for the campaign. Instead, he says the only strategy is to be absolutely authentic so that her voice comes through.

One of the things they began doing was to tweet Vivienne's thoughts. While they also used Facebook, Eric says, "Twitter was the key."

Vivienne began using the tagline "Make a Stand." It turned out, however, that a cyber squatter owned that domain name. When he heard Vivienne's story, he donated the domain to her. He said: "You inspire me. You are giving your lemonade to people, so I am giving this website to you. Thank you, Vivienne."

Over the course of the fall, the Harrs moved Vivienne's campaign from a physical lemonade stand online. Using Fundly, they raised roughly $400,000 by March 1, 2013. The money is being used, in part, to launch a commercially-bottled lemonade, allowing for an infinitely larger scale to combat the problem of child slavery.

Video was key to their success. Eric says they were fortunate to have professional filmmakers volunteer to produce short videos about Vivienne's campaign at no charge. Diane Lam produced a short video of about a minute and Patrick Gilles produced a longer video, over six minutes. The combination of a short video and a longer one proved powerful.

Eric notes that there are nearly 30 million slaves today,

about half of whom are children. In terms of absolute numbers, he says, there have never been more slaves on the planet than there are today.

The Harrs have identified five organization to which they will donate their proceeds: Free The Slaves (bit.ly/GFzKAa), Nepal Youth Foundation (bit.ly/mQcg0M), UNICEF (uni.cf/W3c8k0), the International Programme On The Elimination Of Child Labor (bit.ly/FOq25)—and an organization that focuses on this issue right here in the United States: Gems: Girls Educational & Mentoring Services (bit.ly/9Ct2St).

Vivienne, whose goal is to end child slavery in her lifetime, has a magical way with words for one so young. She says, "Gandhi was one person. Martin Luther King was one person. Mother Teresa was one person. Why can't you be someone who helps?"

CHAPTER 19

INVESTMENT CROWDFUNDING

The world of equity and debt crowdfunding will not likely open to Americans until 2014, but when it does it opens a dramatically bigger opportunity for social entrepreneurs and nonprofits. While nonprofits can't raise equity, they can raise debt—provided they have a clearly demonstrable means to repay it.

Investment crowdfunding was created by Congress and President Obama in the spring of 2012. On April 5, 2012, President Obama signed the JOBS Act, which was passed by Congress with bipartisan support, specifically allowing for businesses to use crowdfunding through FINRA-registered platforms to raise money by issuing equity and debt.

To be clear, we're talking about the sale of securities. This is nearly as different from the rewards-based and donation-based crowdfunding we've been discussing so far as catsup is from mustard. The key difference is that investment crowdfunding is highly regulated. You will have to disclose all of your offering details to the Securities and Exchange Commission through the platform you use.

Don't be discouraged. The premise of the law is that investment crowdfunding must both be easy enough for entrepreneurs to use and regulated enough to protect small investors.

THE JOBS ACT

Three entrepreneurs, Jason Best, Sherwood Neiss, and Zak Cassady-Dorion, who simply thought that investment crowdfunding should be legal, went to the SEC and asked if there wasn't a way it could be done under current law. The SEC explained that it would require an act of Congress. So, they say, "We went and got an act of Congress." They didn't understand that such things are "impossible" and, not understanding that, they got the JOBS Act passed and signed by the president; they were even invited to the White House Rose Garden for the signing. The three ringleaders acknowledge the help of countless others (bit.ly/XLRHaZ).

KEY PROVISIONS OF THE ACT

There may be no better way to communicate the requirements of the law than to literally summarize it here.

It is important to understand some key words in the law.

Issuer: The company or business that raises the money by issuing or selling securities.

Accredited Investor: An accredited investor is one who has a net worth of more than $1 million, excluding the value of the investor's primary residence, or who consistently has an income of over $200,000. Under current law, accredited investors may invest in privately offered securities.

Non-accredited Investor: An investor that does not have either the net worth or income to qualify as an accredited investor. With some narrow exceptions, non-accredited investors are not allowed to invest in privately-offered securities until implementation of the JOBS Act and then it will be subject to the rules of the JOBS Act.

Equity: Equity is a reference to ownership in a business, typically represented by shares of stock. There are many types of stock and not all forms of equity are technically stock. Equity is a broad term that encompasses all forms of equity.

Debt: You know what debt is, of course. Issuers may issue a variety of instruments that are included in debt: bonds, notes, loans, credit lines, commercial paper, etc. As all types of ownership are covered by the term "equity" so are all forms of borrowing covered by the term "debt."

Securities: This is a broad term that encompasses virtually all investment instruments, including debt and equity.

Portal: The Act uses the term portal to refer to the website or platform that acts as an intermediary—the go-between—for the issuance of securities.

Broker-Dealer: A registered broker-dealer is an investment bank that is registered with the SEC and FINRA and acts as an intermediary in these transactions. It is anticipated that they will use online portal-like platforms for their transactions, but as registered broker-dealers they will be allowed to offer more investment advice to investors than mere portals.

The entire Act is just 27 pages long, but only one part, Title III, covers crowdfunding.

The law limits businesses that raise money through crowdfunding to $1 million of crowdfunded investments per twelve-month period. The SEC is likely to clarify when such periods start and end.

Limits are set by the Act on the amount of money non-accredited investors may invest.

- For those with both income and net worth less than $100,000, they will be allowed to invest the greater of $2,000 or 5 percent of the greater of their annual income or net worth.
- For those with either net worth or income greater than $100,000 they will be allowed to invest up to 10 percent of the greater of their annual income or net worth.

The Act requires that all crowdfunded transactions be completed using a registered portal or broker-dealer. You are not allowed to set up your own website to conduct your offering or to use a website like Kickstarter or Indigogo that (as of the time of publication of this book) are not registered with the SEC or FINRA.

The Act also provides some specific rules for intermediaries (portals and broker-dealers). The Act requires that Intermediaries:

- Register with the SEC and FINRA as either a portal or a broker-dealer.
- Provide all of the disclosure of risk that the SEC may require.
- Ensure that investors complete investor education requirements established by the SEC and understand the risks of investing in crowdfunded securities, including the fact that they can lose their entire investment.
- Deter fraud by conducting background checks and taking other measures as required by the SEC.
- Protect the privacy of investors.
- Ensure that investors are not violating their individual investment limits across all of the crowdfunded investments.
- Shall not pay "finders" or "affiliates" of any sort for bringing investors to the opportunities.
- Prohibit its own directors and officers from investing in companies issuing securities on their platforms.

Issuers, that is to say the companies raising money by issuing the new securities, are required by law to disclose the following information (note that the SEC has rulemaking authority to expand and clarify this list):

- Directory information for the company so that people can find and verify its existence.
- Officers, directors and large shareholders (those holding more than 20 percent of the ownership) are required to be disclosed.

- A complete business plan will also be required.
- A description of the financial condition of the company, including tax returns and financial statements.
  - » Those raising less than $100,000, the financial statements needn't be reviewed or audited.
  - » Those raising between $100,000 and $500,000 are required to have their financial statements reviewed.
  - » Finally, those raising more than $500,000 are required to have their financial statements audited.
- Companies must explain the use of "proceeds" or the money raised.
- The price of the securities offered must be disclosed, or, in the event the platform uses an auction or other process to determine a price, the process for setting the price must be disclosed and the price must be made available to investors prior to making a final commitment to participate.
- The ownership structure of the entity must be explained, including the rights of each class of stock so that investors understand how their new shares of ownership (in the case of an equity offering) will compare to the rights of other shareholders.

The Act provides that no one may advertise the terms of the offering. As a result, you won't be allowed to tell your friends the details of the deal, you'll only be allowed to encourage them to read the details using the portal you've selected where they can then get all of the information.

The Act also prohibits issuers from paying people to promote the offering without disclosing that. As a general rule, you should not be paying anyone to promote the sale of your securities outside of the platform itself.

Finally, the Act requires that issuers file annual financial reports with the SEC. Just exactly what that entails will be determined by the SEC.

KEYS TO SUCCESSFUL EQUITY RAISES

With that basic understanding of the rules around investment crowdfunding, let's take a few minutes to talk about some basic tactics for raising equity for your social venture. Remember, if you're running a nonprofit, the community owns it and you cannot sell any part of it—skip ahead to the tips for using crowdfunding for raising money with debt.

Equity crowdfunding is not legal in the U.S., so we have to borrow experiences from markets where it is legal to get a sense of the typical size of a successful raise. It looks like the average is about $100,000; a typical small business crowdfunding raise will be smaller than that, with bigger enterprises that appeal to accredited investors attracting more. Visit TheCrowdCafe.com (bit.ly/11wvgHc) for more data.

This suggests that the average investment will be about $1,500 or about 20 times the average donation of $75 to $80. Most of your investors, however, will invest much less, just a few hundred dollars and a few wealthy friends will skew the average.

If you are content to raise less than $100,000 you should be able to do this with just friends and family. You need to focus on the friends and family members who can write five-digit checks. You may only have a few, but you'll want to get them lined up and committed as early as possible. Their money and influence will help you to get the rest of your money from your friends who'll be investing $500 or $1,000.

Note: as I write this, I keep writing "donate" instead of "invest." The fact is, most businesses fail. That means yours is likely to fail. Make sure that as you raise money from your friends and family that you don't take more money than they can afford to lose in your business and still be able to look you in the eye at Thanksgiving.

If you need to raise more than $100,000, not only will you need to have a CPA firm either review (if you are raising less than $500,000) or audit (if you are raising more than $500,000) your financial statements but you'll also need a different approach.

You'll want to find an angel group (a group of accredited investors that actively seek out private investment opportunities) and work to get them to pledge support for your campaign even before it's launched. Without the support of a large investor or a group of large investors, you will likely struggle to raise the money you want. Most of us simply don't have enough money in our friends and family network to raise hundreds of thousands of dollars.

Don't be discouraged. Remember, you are doing the investors a favor by presenting your deal to them. They need to have lots to choose from in order to find the best investment opportunities. Remember, too, that if they choose to invest in you, they are giving you a big helping hand.

If you are, as I expect, seeking to launch a social venture, you'll want to target angel investors who describe themselves as "impact investors." These are folks who invest with an eye toward both financial returns and to have a social impact.

ABSURDLY SIMPLIFIED VALUATION DISCUSSION

Let me explain that as the head of a boutique investment banking firm, for most of the first decade of this century, I prepared more business valuations than I can count. There are a variety of sophisticated models and approaches that are used to establish business valuations. All of them are done with a thick lacquer of scientific and mathematical analysis. Despite that, valuations for startup businesses are exceptionally subjective.

It comes down to comparing your stage of development and the opportunity in front of you to other businesses that investors have seen at a similar stage of development and opportunity, and comparing the valuation used in the past to help determine a value for your business.

After all is said and done, most deals, from your first friends and family deal to your IPO, will involve you selling from 10 to 40 percent of your business; let's call it 20 percent for sake of simplicity.

The investors know you need to have enough ownership left to be motivated to work on accomplishing your social and financial goals. If they take too much ownership they not only rob you of your motivation but they may make future financing more difficult.

If you sell 20 percent of your business five times in a row you will not have sold 100 percent of your business. Each round that you do involves the sale of new shares, resulting in dilution to the prior shareholders. Angels and Venture capitalists generally ignore the effect of dilution if the value of the business is rising. If the value is dropping, a bigger proportion of the pain of dilution will fall to the founders.

So, if you sell 20 percent of your business five times in a row—to friends and family, to angel investors, to venture capitalists, to private equity investors, and then in an IPO—you should expect to own about 33 percent of the business. If the IPO put the value of your business at $200 million, you'd be worth about $66 million. In other words, you don't have to be afraid of giving up pieces of your company; if you make progress, you'll make millions even if you "give up" much of your company.

Step one toward that objective is a successful friends and family round conducted by crowdfunding.

CROWDFUNDING DEBT

Finally, I'll share a few thoughts about using crowdfunding to borrow money. Every kind of business can borrow money via crowdfunding—even nonprofits. Remember, however, that unlike soliciting donations or offering rewards, when you borrow money you are issuing securities so you are required to do that on a registered platform or through a broker-dealer.

The loans you get using crowdfunding will likely require a higher rate of interest than corporations get when they borrow money from big banks. Of course, you are not a large corporation. Chances are good that you may not be able to borrow any money for your business from a bank.

The interest rates you pay should also be lower than credit card rates. In other words, expect to pay anywhere between high single-digit interest rates to rates in the high teens.

Because a registered platform is prohibited from providing investment advice, lending platforms that are not run by broker-dealers will not be allowed to provide advice on the pricing of interest rates on loans. That will mean that interest rates will either be set one-to-one by the borrowers and lenders or the platform will create a mechanism for all of the interested lenders to work together to settle on a rate—without input from the platform.

Broker-dealers, in contrast, will be allowed to offer investment advice and may choose to be actively involved in setting the interest rate between borrowers and lenders.

For startup businesses of any sort, borrowing money is generally not workable. Without a history proving an ability to repay debt, you'll be forced to focus on donations and/or equity.

For businesses with a few years of history with positive cash flow, debt will prove to be a primary tool for capitalizing or funding your business. Crowdfunding will make borrowing money possible for a large group of small businesses for which borrowing money has been virtually impossible.

For additional information regarding investment crowdfunding, I recommend the book *Crowdfund Investing for Dummies* (amzn.to/12ITT7z) by Sherwood Neiss, Jason Best and Zak Cassady-Dorion.

CHAPTER 20

EMPOWER YOUR VOLUNTEERS TO SHARE THE MESSAGE

Dave McMurtry is a player in Silicon Valley. I mean that in the very best sense. He is a graduate of the Stanford Graduate School of Business and has spent much of his career in the tech community, including more than half a decade at tech giant Intuit. He more recently served as the CEO of Loomia, a social media company.[15]

In 2005, Dave wanted to take a break from his career to give back. As a pilot, his first choice was to volunteer some flight time to Doctors without Borders, but when he found out there weren't any of those volunteer opportunities available at that time he decided his help was needed more elsewhere.[16]

He called several prominent nonprofits to volunteer his time in experimenting—and in 2005 that's what crowdfunding was—with the idea of using social media to raise money for

15 http://www.linkedin.com/in/davemcmurtry (linkd.in/13AvCz9)

16 Most of the information for this article came from an interview with David McMurtry on April 2, 2013.

nonprofits. He says, "No one knew what to do with me."

Dave McMurtry in Colombia

In July 2004, Dave had served as a volunteer supporting official U.N. observers for the first elections in Afghanistan. While there, he and some of his colleagues helped build a home for a local who was working with them. Dave saw first-hand the impact that having a home had on this man and his family.

Drawing on this experience, and as a longtime volunteer at Habitat for Humanity Silicon Valley, he tried Habitat for Humanity International, offering to create a crowdfunding initiative for a specific project without any resources from the organization. Jonathan Reckford, the CEO, quickly accepted Dave's offer to volunteer his time and fully fund the experiment. They agreed to run the project in Colombia, which Dave describes as one of his "favorites," so Dave flew there to launch the experiment.

The project was to build and fund five homes at a total cost of $25,000. Dave quickly raised $200,000 so the project was dramatically expanded, ultimately putting 250 homeless people, displaced by the terrible violence in the region, back into housing.

The success of the program helped to change the relationship between Habitat for Humanity in Colombia and the government of Colombia, which has since become a major funding mechanism.

After this successful experiment in 2005, Dave went back to the corporate world as the CEO of Loomia.

Upon leaving Loomia, he volunteered for several months with Kiva, working in Liberia in support of their microfinance programs. Making the world a better place is what drives Dave.

In 2009, Habitat CEO Jonathan Reckford called Dave to ask him to come to join the cause full time to lead the effort to create an aspirational five-year strategic plan and also to "run with this crowdfunding idea."

Over the past year, Habitat has raised more than $1 million on the Share.Habitat platform, powered by Fundly, proving the vitality of crowdfunding. Dave believes Habitat will raise a multiple of that number in 2013.

Given Habitat's success, I asked Dave to share some of his ideas for best practices.

His first rule is to empower the volunteers to share the story. He says, "Empower the volunteer to have the same capabilities as the organization's marketing and PR teams to speak passionately in the first voice about the mission." In large organizations this can be challenging because so much is invested in the brand, but he suggests that success comes from truly empowering the volunteers to do the work because they strengthen and embolden the brand.

Second, the volunteers should be invited to take responsibility for their success and then must be given credit for it.

The third key, he says, is "rich story telling." You must give your volunteers tools to enable them to tell their story about your cause in a powerful way. Give them the ability to upload and share photos and videos to help them communicate their passion.

After joining Habitat full time, Dave met David Boyce, the CEO and founder of Fundly. Habitat now uses the Fundly platform for its fundraising efforts on Share.Habitat.org. Fundly has the tools to allow volunteers set up their own fundraising pages, giving volunteers the power McMurtry sought to put them front and center.

On the success of the Habitat for Humanity campaign, Boyce said, "Habitat's secret for building a sustainable, high-growth crowdfunding program is the marriage of online and offline experiences. Habitat was able to create a compelling offline experience (home building) and attach to that experience a fundraising requirement. Because people want the experience and are committed to the mission, they are willing to fundraise in order to participate."[17]

17 David Boyce was interviewed via email for this story.

ADDENDA

SHAUN KING BRINGS HOPE(MOB) TO CROWDFUNDING

This article appeared on Forbes.com (onforb.es/10heW9Z) on March 28, 2013.

Shaun King

Shaun King, founder of the nonprofit HopeMob is revolutionizing crowdfunding for social good with his web site that, unlike most crowdfunding platforms, actually comes with a crowd.

Born in Kentucky in a working class family, as a fifteen-year-old he was beaten so badly in what was one of the first registered hate crimes in the state that he needed a series of surgeries that required two years. He notes, "When bad things happen to some people it hardens their heart, but for me it softened my heart." He attended Morehouse College where Martin Luther King had attended and was required to do service.

While at Morehouse, using bulletin boards and chat rooms, King began using technology to rally people to volunteer for causes.

When he graduated, he took a job teaching civics and continued using technology to help nonprofit organizations. Eventually, his career morphed until he became a technology consultant for nonprofits.

In 2008, he became a pastor in Atlanta. He visited an inner-city school and promised that his church would provide each student a toy and a new uniform. He didn't appreciate that it would cost $55,000–money the church didn't have.

In the earliest days of Twitter, he used the social network to raise the money.

His work caught the attention of the media and in 2009 he raised $1 million for flood relief in Atlanta and organized 10,000 volunteers there. In January 2010, the earthquake in Haiti caught his attention and he raised $1 million for relief there.

He then created HopeMob, to make it easy for people to give to a cause or to people in need. HopeMob has now raised more than $5 million for causes of all sorts. HopeMob is different from other crowdfunding sites, he says.

"If you don't have your own social network it's almost impossible to raise money on other crowdfunding sites." At HopeMob, Shaun and his team are actively involved in vetting the stories to validate the needs and then they help to write up the story and bring the money from the HopeMob.

HopeMob has over 450,000 followers on Twitter and 113,000 likes on Facebook. In addition, everyone who signs up at HopeMob.com will get email notifications of people in need. While many crowdfunding platforms are better described as peerfunding platforms where you bring your peers, HopeMob brings the crowd.

In addition, HopeMob doesn't charge any fees to the fundraiser. Every dollar raised for a campaign on the site, goes to the campaign. At check out, donors are asked to volunteer to pay a little extra to help cover these costs. Corporations sometimes "sponsor" a campaign and cover the costs. HopeMob is also working with Dwolla to reduce transaction costs; Dwolla charges just $0.25 per bank transfer over $25 and waives the fee entirely for transfers under $25.

Shaun wants HopeMob to become all that crowdfunding promises to be for those in need.

CROWDFUNDING FOR BOSTON MARATHON VICTIMS SHOWS SUPPORT FROM AROUND THE WORLD

This article appeared on Forbes.com (onforb.es/17oZLPN) on April 17, 2013.

Sydney and Celeste Corcoran

Among the 170 wounded near the finish line of the Boston Marathon on Monday were Celeste and Sydney Corcoran, mother and daughter there to see her sister Carmen finish the race on Monday.

Celeste lost both legs in the bombing and Sydney whose injuries were life threatening is expected to recover fully. Both women had additional surgeries today and anticipate more before their battle for recovery is complete.

Cousin to Celeste, Alyssa Carter reports that both women are in good spirits, with Celeste joking about becoming the "next Blade Runner."

Alyssa, anxious to rally support for the family in the face of devastating emotional and financial costs associated with the treatment, recovery and long-term implications of the terrible injuries launched a crowdfunding campaign on the site GoFundMe.

Alyssa chose GoFundMe after talking to colleagues at work where she is involved in "online marketing." An executive of her firm recommended the site, but before making a final selection she set up accounts on several sites, finally choosing GoFundMe for its ease of use and reputation. "I tried to think of someone like my Dad using it," she says.

In just over 24 hours, $206,005 has been donated to the fund by nearly 3,000 people from across the country and around the world, with donations coming from as far away as Australia. The campaign got off to a quick start, Alyssa explains, with their "large Catholic family." Once they all put out the word on Facebook and Twitter, the donations started to roll in immediately.

Sydney's sister Carmen was stopped about half a mile before the finish line when the blasts ended the race. According to Alyssa, Celeste has seemed more disappointed not to have seen Carmen finish the race than to have lost her legs.

Alyssa notes on the campaign page that they are still looking to identify the heroes who saved Sydney's life: "We are still trying to locate the heroes who helped at the scene as doctors believe they saved Sydney's life. Many of you have seen the pictures of Sydney. I won't post the pictures here, but can email them by request. There is one man in a plaid shirt, one with a grey t-shirt and blue baseball cap, and one with a red t-shirt which was used as a tourniquet on Sydney's leg. We owe them unspeakable gratitude."

HOW TO RAISE $16 MILLION FROM CROWDFUNDING IN ONE DAY

This article appeared on Forbes.com (onforb.es/ZLVLYX) on March 13, 2013.

Minnesota's GiveMN raised $16.3 million in one day using crowdfunding site Razoo in November of 2012. In what has become a major annual event in the nonprofit community in Minnesota, 4,381 nonprofits participated, raising money from 53,339 people on "Give to the Max Day."

The Community Foundation of Utah (with whom I volunteer) is sponsoring and organizing the Love UT Give UT campaign which will happen on March 22, 2013 with hopes of raising over $1 million for nearly 400 participating nonprofits.

Fraser Nelson, Executive Director of the Community Foundation of Utah notes that Utah is a unique state, saying, "We are the most charitable state in the nation, by far. Utahns give on average 10.6% of their income to charity and are consistently #1 in hours of volunteer service. While much of those funds go to faith organizations, it creates a culture of giving. We are the youngest state, among the most 'wired', and are heavy users of social media."

Utah's Nelson adds, "In all these ways Love UT Give UT makes particular sense for Utah. It is easy, it is high tech, and it is in line with our values of giving back while recognizing our increasing diversity. I know we'll see that in full force on March 22."

Razoo exclusively serves nonprofits in their online fundraising efforts and has helped them raise approximately $139 million. Razoo has hosted many of these community-wide fund raising days. Minnesota presently holds the record, but the Dallas, Texas community is not far behind.

Razoo CEO Lesley Mansford offers the following tips for successful community led fundraising campaigns:

1. **Incentivize the behavior you want to see, both the behavior of donors and of nonprofits:** encourage creativity.
2. **Use effective partnerships:** leverage media, nonprofit groups, and local PR firms to amplify the message of the day and rally their networks to collective action.
3. **Train your nonprofits:** teach them how to use social media, help them cultivate long-term relationships with donors; show them how they can tell the story of the work they do. The more prepared and confident your nonprofits are, the better the giving experience will be, and the more donors will enjoy giving and so do it more often."

Dana Nelson (no relation to her Utah counterpart), the Executive Director of GiveMN, the person primarily responsible for the world record for single-day fundraising offers these tips for success:

1. **Matching grants:** With Razoo it is easy to add to the page and easy for donors to find nonprofits with matching grants so their money can be leveraged. It is vitally important for nonprofits to go out and find their own matching grants.

2. **Be creative:** Nonprofits must engage in competition, find ways to stand out by doing fun things. As an example of this creativity, we have a local arts organization that live streamed 24 hours of improv, another allowed donors to write a line in a play that was later performed.
3. **Spread the word:** Each organization must reach out to boards, employees, fans, followers and supporters to spread the link both in advance and on the day.

Utah's Nelson also offered her advice based on what she's learned so far from organizing the Love UT Give UT day of giving scheduled for next week, saying, "This is a shared responsibility of the corporate, nonprofit, and education sectors and we are in the role of community organizer, booster and funder. It takes a lot of hands. We cannot control - nor do we want to - the events in local communities and businesses, the ways participating organizations are getting the word out. Next year we'll have a much better idea of how one of these works, but my advice is remember this is about and for the community. It really is about love - our collective love of place, people and causes."

One of the key ways that GiveMN motivated its nonprofits was through contests. The number of donors to each nonprofit is tracked in real time by Razoo, allowing the nonprofits to compete for the most donors. Cash prizes were given to dozens of nonprofits based on their number of donors. A $12,500 first prize was given in four categories: all nonprofits, medium (nonprofits with budgets from $100,000 to $1 million), small (nonprofits with budgets of less than $100,000), and higher education. In each category a $5,000 second prize, a $2,500 third prize and $1,000 prizes for 4th through 10th place were given.

With an average raised of just under $3,000 per organization, the prizes were significant and motivated the nonprofits to meaningfully engage their base to expand their reach on Give to the Max Day.

Razoo's Mansfield shared how she feels her role in raising so much money for nonprofits, saying, "It's both personally and professionally rewarding that we can raise millions of dollars in a single day for the nonprofits of a region and drive greater awareness of the amazing work they are doing in the local community. I feel so proud that the technology we have built can have such an impact on the day itself and also provide the nonprofits with a new set of tools they can use as part of their fundraising toolkit year round."

Other giving days coming up include "Match Day Milwaukee" on March 14, 2013, "Arizona Gives Day" on March 20, 2013, "Nevada Gives" on April 25, 2013, "Spring 2 Action Alexandria" on April 17, 2013, "Live PC Give PC" on November 8, 2013. The next GiveMN Give to the Max day will be November 14, 2013.

CROWDFUNDING IS ABOUT CREATING JOBS FOR THE RIGHT PEOPLE

This article appeared on Forbes.com (onforb.es/Y9oWVc) on February 20, 2013.

Crowdfunding is not just about creating jobs, it is about creating jobs for the right people. In April of 2012, President Obama signed the JOBS Act into law, authorizing crowdfunding of equity and debt for the sake of creating jobs. The more time I spend studying crowdfunding and working with the leaders in the crowdfund community, the clearer it becomes that not only will crowdfunding create jobs, it will create jobs in the right places.

Candace Klein speaking at the National Press Club

Recently, I sat down in a hidden valley near Park City, Utah with Candace Klein, CEO of Somolend and founder of the nonprofit Bad Girl Ventures, who explained that overwhelmingly, the people were polled about crowdfunding indicating a desire to raise capital are women, African Americans and Hispanic Americans. In other words, crowdfunded capital will flow to entrepreneurs in the communities that have been most disadvantaged in America.

According to Klein, women own over 50 percent of the businesses in the United States but receive less than 5 percent of "traditional capital" and less than 3 percent of venture capital. Klein notes that she founded Bad Girl Ventures specifically to address this problem. BGV has funded 45 women-owned businesses with a total of $5 million, but also had to turn away thousands of women. This inspired Klein to launch Somolend so that she could provide capital to thousands of women owned businesses. This also allows "women investors to build their own wealth," she notes.

Furthermore, according to Klein, Somolend is already doing lending, matching both banks and individuals to small borrowers, 40 percent of whom are nonprofits. The pricing for debt is set on an individual basis between the borrower and lender. The rates range between 3 and 22 percent. Multiple lenders may participate in the same loan to one borrower at different rates. The borrowers send the payment to Somolend, which then remits the corresponding payments to each of the borrowers.

Klein's Somolend exemplifies the potential of crowdfunding to allocate capital more efficiently to the very people who are locked out of current capital markets, creating jobs in communities that have not been participating in the growth of the U.S. economy since 2000. In addition, the capital being allocated to nonprofits expands the good they can do.

Yesterday, I reconnected with Candace in Washington, DC. She joined her peers from the Crowdfund Intermediary Regulatory Advocates to lobby for implementation of crowdfunding anticipated in the 2012 law—which still awaits SEC and FINRA regulations. Rumors are rampant that the draft regulations are ready—and have been for months—but that the politics of the appointment of the new head of the SEC has led to a delay in issuing the regulations for comment.

Jason Best and Sherwood Niess, of Crowdfund Capital Advisors, who led the lobbying effort for the JOBS Act and were recognized by President Obama in the Rose Garden ceremony last year, were there to lead the effort to call for action from the SEC. They were joined by their partner, Judy Robinette; Vincent Molinari, CEO of GATE Technologies; Karen Kerrigan, CEO of the Small Business and Entrepreneurship Council; Doug Ellenoff, partner at Ellenoff, Grossman and Schole; Sara Hanks, CEO of Crowd Check; Kim Wales, CEO of Wales Capital, Chance Barnett, CEO of Crowdfunder; Chris Tyrell, Principal of Nehemiah Investments, Ryan Feit, CEO of Seed Invest and, of course, Klein, who helped draft the JOBS Act.

Jason Best with Sherwood Neiss at the National Press Club

The group met with congressional staff on Capitol Hill and later met with a coterie of senior staff and Senators in the White House to press the issue.

Some notable remarks from the group include:

Robinette said, "Crowdfunding is not just an economic issue, it is a women's issue. It is also an African American issue. In fact, crowdfunding represents the greatest democratization of small business capital in history. While venture capital is allocated almost exclusively to businesses owned by men, crowdfunding is already being allocated in nearly perfect proportion to the composition of our population."

Judy Robinett presenting at the National Press Club

Neiss said, "In the 320 days since the President signed the JOBS Act into law a vibrant crowdfunding industry has formed to live up to the promise of Title III - access to capital with prudent investor protections. We are here today to showcase for Washington how we are ready to embark on Web 3.0, where social media meets community financing. We hope the demonstration of this robust trade association will give the SEC the confidence it needs to release the proposed rules so America's Job creators can get the capital they need to innovate and grow."

Kerrigan said, "The capital needs of entrepreneurs remain just as critical as when the JOBS Act was signed last April. The build out and investment that has gone into creating an efficient, transparent and accessible marketplace for small businesses to find needed capital and protect investors is extraordinary. Now, the SEC must take the next step and finalize its rulemakings so the JOBS Act can fulfill its promise of helping fund promising businesses, creating jobs and bringing the economy back to robust levels of growth."

Feit said, "I am excited to demo Seed-Invest's crowdfunding platform on Capitol Hill in order illustrate the massive potential the JOBS Act has to transform early-stage financing. We need to ensure that lawmakers are proud of the burgeoning industry they spawned and that they do not lose sight of how crucial crowdfunding is for startups and small businesses."

Ryan Feit presenting at the National Press Club

Best and Niess, for their part, are taking their show on the road. They are traveling the world helping other countries to implement reasoned laws for doing crowdfunding. Of course, Australia and the UK, among a handful of countries, have already implemented crowdfunding, allow the U.S. to analyze their experiences to determine best practices.

If you would like to get involved with advocating for the crowdfunding industry, please join the Crowdfunding Professional Association.

TOP TEN ISSUES RAISED AT TEXAS CROWDFUNDING CONFERENCE

This article appeared on Forbes.com on January 9, 2013.

The CrowdfundTX Conference featured an impressive assemblage of crowdfunding leaders from around the country. Organizer, Chris Camillo Founding Board Member of the Crowdfunding Professionals Association, noted that bringing this group of "speakers together may never happen again." The conference kept participants glued to their seats as real issues were discussed, leaving everyone feeling updated and excited about investment crowdfunding.

Chris Camillo

The top ten issues discussed at the conference were:

Jobs: Investment crowdfunding was approved in 2012 when President Obama signed the JOBS Act into law; implementation still awaits regulations from the SEC and FINRA. The jobs, however, aren't waiting. Heather Lopes, CEO of EarlyShares, noted that the "JOBS Act has already created 1,500 to 2,000 jobs" from firms that have been launched to do investment crowdfunding and provide related services since the law passed. This represents a mere drop in the bucket compared to the potential jobs impact from unleashing investment crowdfunding, panelists suggested.

Investment Crowdfunding: Perks or reward-based crowdfunding arguably goes back hundreds of years though its popularity on the internet goes back only about five years. Camillo noted that some companies can make little use of rewards-based crowdfunding, suggesting that a "If a physician has an idea for a new medical device, that is a better fit for equity." Lopes also noted that the kindness that led to a New York community raising $75,000 to help a restaurant destroyed by Hurricane Sandy will also influence equity investments in crowdfunding.

Race and Gender: Visiting one-on-one with Jonathan Sandlund of TheCrowdCafe while being filmed for a segment in the upcoming documentary film Crowd of Angels, Sandlund agreed that crowdfunding would largely eliminate cultural biases observed in angel and venture capital financing, which are dominated by men making investments in businesses controlled by men. Crowdfunding deals go to women in the roughly the same proportion that women own businesses, according to The Crowdfunding Revolution. Sandlund expressed the belief that racial bias is also being eliminated by crowdfunding. Rodney Sampson, author of Kingonomics, said, "If you don't know what crowdfunding is, you can't seek it out. We need an onramp of over-, over-education." He added that for venture capitalists, crowdfunding "success will come first; race and gender will become secondary."

Regulations for Title II: The SEC is required to issue regulations governing both Titles II and III of the JOBS Act. Title II relates to new rules for the general solicitation of offerings for accredited investors. Panelists Candace Klein, CEO of SomoLend; Maurice Lopes, founder of EarlyShares; DJ Paul, founder of Crowdfunder; Scott Purcell, founder of Arctic Island; and Kim Wales, of Wales Capital reached a loose consensus that regulation for Title II would be completed before the regulations for the more anticipated Title III provisions related to consumer crowdfunding. Wales was essentially alone in her optimistic view that regulations would be issued either late in the first quarter or early in the second quarter.

Regulations for Title III: The same panel concluded that regulations for crowdfunding won't likely be issued by the SEC and FINRA before the end of the third quarter or possibly into the fourth quarter. Klein praised the regulators, saying, "We love the SEC." Most agreed that the SEC has worked in a spirit of cooperation to establish the rules required by the JOBS Act.

Deal Size: Rewards based crowdfunding campaigns, according to Brian Meece and Jed Cohen, founders of RocketHub, typically range from $3,500 to $35,000. Sandlund said that data from CrowdCube, and equity platform in the U.K., had an average deal size of $88,000, suggesting that the average equity deal would be about four to five times as large as the typical rewards-based crowdfunding campaign.

Brian Meece and Jed Cohen

Costs: Maurice Lopes, founder of EarlyShares, said to expect platforms to charge "5 to 10 percent" of funds raised to cover the costs of issuing shares through crowdfunding. Doug Ellenoff of Ellenoff, Grossman and Schole, noted that with legal and accounting fees, the costs could reach as high as "20 percent" of the proceeds. Of course, several panelists noted that such calculations were dependent on a wide variety of factors including the size of the offering.

International Crowdfunding: Jason Best, of Crowdfund Capital Advisors, said, "Make no mistake, crowdfunding is a global movement. While the U.S. still represents the largest market for crowdfunding, Carl Espositi of Crowdfunder.org noted that the number of crowdfunding platforms, while smaller in Europe, they are "growing at twice the rate of the U.S." Sandlund also observed that investment crowdfunding is legal in Australia and the U.K., among other countries. He noted that the U.K. site FundingCircle funded two $80,000 loans in under 29 minutes. Best also noted that because charging interest is prohibited under Islamic law, "The Muslim world is working to implement equity crowdfunding."

Heather Lopes

Crowdfund History: Sherwood Neiss, of Crowdfund Capital Advisors, described the naiveté with which he and Jason Best approached Washington to begin lobbying for the passage of the JOBS Act. He said, "We literally started knocking on doors asking to speak with the representatives and Senators; people looked at us like we were nuts. So, we asked, 'Who is in charge of jobs?'" They're naïve approach ultimately worked with their legislation passing the House with overwhelming bipartisan support and a vote of 407-17. Their coordination of industry leaders working with the SEC and FINRA through the Crowdfunding Intermediaries Regulatory Association demonstrates how much they've learned in a short period of time.

Fraud: One theme that came up several times during the day is the fear of regulators and some detractors of crowdfunding about the potential for fraud at the expense of small investors. Sandlund noted that in a careful review of $250 million of crowdfunding transactions, he found not a single case of fraud. Ellenoff said, "Crowdfunding is at worst friends and family financing done better." He pointed out that the use of crowdfunding platforms will enhance transparency and accountability for transactions that are happening to some degree anyway.

Richard Seline, a native Texan and former advisor to President George H.W. Bush, said, "Texans don't like to finish second." It is clear that Texas is ready for crowdfunding; the question is when will crowdfunding be ready for Texas?

CROWDFUNDING SUCCESS STORIES INCLUDE $35,000 FOR SOCK MONKEYS AND $2,000 FOR A DRY COMPOSTING TOILET

This article appeared on Forbes.com (onforb.es/WzOifW) on January 30, 2013.

Social entrepreneurs of all varieties are turning to crowdfunding to launch or expand their social efforts; recently I've connected with five who have shared their stories of how they raised up to $100,000 each.

Do Good Bus Tour, Las Vegas Rescue Mission

Rebecca Pontius led the effort for an organization called the Do Good Bus to raise $100,000 on StartSomeGood to show people how to volunteer by taking them on a bus to volunteer all around the country. She said, "A friend and I had been volunteering in LA for the past ten years at a couple different organizations and consistently had friends ask, 'How do you know where to volunteer? How do you get involved?' So we decided to put all those questioning friends on a bus and SHOW them exactly how to volunteer."

Martha Griffin raised $31,763 on Kickstarter to publish a children's book called Sam's Birthmark. "When our son Barron was born with a port wine stain on his face," she says, she was inspired to write the book. "Every child in the world is unique and special in their own way, and certain special characteristics make them shine as an individual. We want to show this message through a book with the child having a birthmark."

Jennifer Windrum raised $35,000 on StartSomeGood for SMAC—Sock Monkeys Against Cancer. "My Mom, Leslie Lehrman, is the inspiration behind the creation of SMAC! She lived more than 1,200 miles away, making her appointments, tests, scan results and treatments that much harder for both of us. I wanted to give her something she could have, hold and touch when I couldn't be with her. I created SMAC! to give Mom a "buddy" she could hug to remind her that I am with her," she says.

SMAC! Sock Monkey

Kristopher Young, head of PROViDE, which provides care for people in Haiti, raised over $2,000 on StartSomeGood for a dry composting toilet. "We reached our goal plus with very little effort," he says.

Brad Hurvitz, founder of Trek to Teach, raised $2,910 on StartSomeGood. "I had an opportunity to teach in a boarding school in Rajasthan, India through a connection of my brother. The challenge of going to an extremely foreign country and the opportunity of giving back was a perfect combination for me to satisfy the desire I had within. While there, I taught English to grades 4, 5, and 6. I was the soccer coach, photography teacher, taught kids how to swim, trained students for a marathon, helped market the boarding school and I directed the school's first play, Pygmalion. I will never forget the expressions upon the faces of my students and had never felt such true gratification in my life," he says.

These successful social entrepreneurs have offered some insights from their successes that are relevant for anyone wishing to raise money through crowdfunding.

Jennifer Windrum, a PR/social media strategist (turned activist) created a full marketing strategy for her campaign. "As a one-man band," she says, "I had to continually re-prioritize aspects of the strategy, as I couldn't possibly tackle all that I wanted to. I needed to build an army. So, part of that strategy included building a private group of ambassadors on Facebook who could follow, and be an active part of the campaign from the very beginning, such as watching the making of the prototypes, trying to find a manufacturer - all the details it took to bring the SMAC! monkeys and the campaign to launch. Once the campaign kicked-off, this group had a very vested interest, an emotional connection, to these little monkeys and worked to help make them a reality."

She adds, "While this was primarily an online campaign, I also took it offline, where those who aren't plugged into the social media world could participate by holding SMAC!-downs. A SMAC!-down is basically a girl's night out with a social good twist. I livestreamed a SMAC!-down at my house to officially kick off the campaign. I set up laptops where people could pledge right then and there, while they ate, drank and mingled. I provided language and directions on how others across the country could host SMAC!-downs...and they did."

Her strategy paid off, she says, "According to StartStomeGood, the SMAC! campaign opened with the highest-earning first day in the history of the crowdfunding platform, raising over $5,000 within 24 hours."

Brad Hurvitz noted, "Alex (Budak of StartSomeGood) and I had a discussion about the most effective fundraising strategy using their crowdfunding platform. He told me that the video was the most important part. Organize it like an essay: intro, body and conclusion. He told me to clearly communicate my mission and ASK for support and not to make it longer than 3 minutes!" He then recruited a professional video editor to help with the video on a pro bono basis.

Kristopher Young advised, "In my experience, having specific goals, funding amounts, and a timeline are integral parts to crowdfunding successes." He added, "Our entire campaign was focused on the Facebook community and a small list of donors in our email contact database. We set our goal amount, an ending date for the campaign, and posted reminders occasionally on Facebook and sent two emails to everyone in our database during a 3-week campaign."

Rebecca Pontius says, "We raised just over $100,000 on StartSomeGood to take the Do Good Bus on tour with the band Foster The People." She adds, "It took consistent monitoring, posts on Twitter and Facebook, personal begging emails to friends and support from the band to raise the money in time." She also observed that choosing the right platform is key. She originally launched her campaign on Kickstarter but was "booted" because the project wasn't a creative project; she quickly switched to StartSomeGood where she was successful.

Martha Griffin reported, "Our goal was $25,000 and we raised $31,763 on Kickstarter to publish a children's book called Sam's Birthmark. We sent numerous e-mail campaigns to our friends, family and our entire network. We also heavily targeted friends of friends and the Vascular Birthmark community through Facebook."

Comparing notes across these efforts, it is fair to conclude that raising money for social entrepreneurship is like raising money for almost anything else. It is easy to raise a bit of money and an organized, concerted effort and a large existing network, community or fan base is required to raise a lot of money through crowdfunding.

CROWDFUNDING TO THE RESCUE FOLLOWING SUPERSTORM SANDY

This article appeared on Forbes.com (onforb.es/U4YhZF) on November 2, 2012.

Rina, a mother of five living right on the water in Sheepshead Bay in the Brooklyn borough of New York City had her home flooded in Superstorm Sandy and was forced to evacuate without knowing when she could return. By Friday, November 02, 2012, a friend living in the relative safety of the Bronx has raised over $3,000 of emergency cash for Rina and her kids by setting up a crowdfunding page at GoFundMe.com.

Retired Brooklyn Tech High School football coach, "DiBo" DiBenedetto lost his home in Belle Harbor, New York to a fire that reportedly damaged or destroyed more than twenty homes in the storm and Malcolm Davis, a football coach at Xaverian High School set up a page at GoFundMe.com that raised over $15,000 in 48 hours to help the coach start over.

Kate O'Sullivan launched a GoFundMe page to help those in her neighborhood of Rockaway Beach in the borough of Queens New

York on Wednesday; by Friday afternoon, she'd raised over $6,000 to buy generators and other emergency supplies—well ahead of the arrival of help from the Red Cross or FEMA. She was in Boston during the storm and was able to buy supplies there, rent a U-haul and get them to New York.

Rebecca Zinger, who set up the page for Rina and her children, explained, "I'm only doing this because I'm like a sister [to Rina] and I love her." She set up the page on GoFundMe initially hoping only to raise $500, but when that goal was quickly surpassed, she raised the goal to $5,000. In just one day she's raised over $3,000 for Rina, whose oldest recently turned 13 and just celebrated his Bar Mitzvah.

Rina with her children, recently celebrating the Bar Mitzvah of her oldest son

For her part, Rebecca says the storm howled fiercely through her Bronx neighborhood, but the worst she suffered was "losing cable for five minutes."

Malcolm Davis, the football coach who started the campaign for Coach Dibenedetto explained that he'd worked for the now retired coach years ago and played for him early in the elder coach's career. Malcolm says, "I've been a football player all of my life. I'm a good football player. Good football players make plays, they make an impact." When he heard what had happened to his dear friend Coach Dibo, he thought "something has to be done." He decided, "I'm going to rally the troops." He launched a campaign on Facebook. There, Ahmed Shama, a former player and U.S. Marine told him about GoFundMe and Coach Davis quickly launched the page.

Coach "Dibo" DiBenedetto

Coach Davis has been proactive about raising the money, noting, "I don't take 'no' for an answer."

On the page set up for football coach DiBenedetto, the coach writes, "It's overwhelming to see and read this outpouring of love that I am receiving from the people who are great friends and are very dear to me. The things we have shared and the challenges we have faced together as football players, choral students, colleagues and friends give me the strength to move forward and meet this latest challenge in my life with a firm resolve."

Kate O'Sullivan, who launched the page to help the folks in her neighborhood of Rockaway Beach promises to give all of the money to help her and her neighbors rebuild. She says everyone in the neighborhood comprised mostly of civil servants--teachers, cops and firemen--is working together and helping each other. Kate wanted to shout out her appreciation, saying, "Thank you to the sanitation department," which she says has been especially great in the early days.

GoFundMe CEO Brad Damphousse tells me, "We built GoFundMe to be the place where family, friends and communities come together and support one another when they need it most. Americans know that real charity starts at home, not in the offices of government agencies. GoFundMe empowers individuals to take immediate action and do the right thing when others are in need. We're honored and humbled to play a small role as thousands of regular people are coming together to accomplish amazing things for those affected by Hurricane Sandy. Our thoughts and prayers are with all those whose lives are forever changed as a result of this storm."

GoFundMe isn't the only site offering people the chance to raise money to organize their own disaster relief. HelpersUnite.com is another site where disaster victims can create a profile and request help. HelpersUnite is owned by EarlyShares.

Stephen Temes, Chairman and Co-Founder of EarlyShares, said by email, "Having lived the majority of my life in New York City, the devastation that the North East is now facing after Hurricane Sandy really hits home. This hurricane is something that will take more than a while to recover from and we want to make sure that families have a way to reach out to their friends and loved ones for targeted support to help get their lives back on track. These people will need help dealing with the destruction that Hurricane Sandy has caused. As the initial shock subsides, the damage will remain and these families will still need long-term help. The ability as time goes on for these families to draw from their network of friends, family, community, and anyone else for financial support via our social giving platform will make a real difference for those that need it the most."

Please share your experiences raising money or donating money for Superstorm Sandy relief efforts in the comments below.

If you are interested in helping me with my research for a forthcoming book on crowdfunding for social entrepreneurs, please click here. Those who participate in the survey will receive a free download of my book, Your Mark On The World.

Please help me continue this conversation on Twitter at @devindthorpe and on Facebook, Google+ and at my personal website yourmarkontheworld.com.

FOUR CROWDFUNDING MISTAKES FOR SOCIAL ENTREPRENEURS TO AVOID

This article appeared on Forbes.com (onforb.es/VlnFoE) on December 5, 2012.

A few weeks ago, I ran into an entrepreneur who said, "I tried raising money on [a crowdfunding platform] but it didn't work." I'm sure he's not the only one who's had that experience. Crowdfunding isn't a magic well of money. It's just a new way to raise it.

Recently, I've connected with a number of successful social entrepreneurs and crowdfunders to learn more about common mistakes that social entrepreneurs make.

Unrealistic expectations: Andrea Lo, CEO of Piggybackr, observes that a big crowdfunding mistake is "Unrealistic expectations in relation to setting high goals and expectations for press. People anchor to the long tail of projects they hear about in the media that raise millions of dollars. The reality is the average project raises just a couple thousand dollars just from friends and family. When reality doesn't meet expectation, crowdfunders and supporters alike lose momentum." She concludes, "It's better to reach a lower goal and exceed it rather than set a really high goal and not even get close even if you raise the same amount."

"Build it and they will come": Piers Duruz, Founder of KickstarterHQ (not affiliated with Kickstarter, Inc.) notes that a common mistake is "Taking an 'If you build it (a project page on a crowdfunding site) they will come,' [approach] without putting any thought into marketing it."

Marketing: David Boyce, Founder and Customer Experience Officer at Fundly, notes that "Crowdfunding is a very powerful mechanism for funding social good, but many social entrepreneurs overestimate its power. The biggest mistake I see social entrepreneurs make with crowdfunding is to underinvest in marketing their campaign. It is tempting to believe that if you have written brilliant copy about an incredible initiative and uploaded that copy, along with photos and videos, onto a gorgeous crowdfunding page, people will be impressed and begin to fund your venture. What people, exactly, are going to do this? You have to get the word out before anyone at all sees your campaign. It's like throwing a party. You can get the right caterer, DJ and venue, but if you don't send out invitations, you won't have a very good party. And if you don't keep the momentum building toward the date of your party, you may also not have a great party." He concludes, "You have to market like crazy to throw a good party, and you have to market like crazy to run a good crowdfunding campaign."

David Boyce, Fundly

Small donations: Chris Camillo, a Texas super angel, author of *Laughing at Wall Street* and the producer of an upcoming documentary on crowdfunding, says a big mistake he sees is "Not actively soliciting small dollar pledges. An actively engaged donor who pledges just

$1 while making a personal plea on your behalf to their 1000 person Facebook/Twitter network could turn out to be more valuable than an inactive donor who pledges $50."

There are some projects that may not be a good fit for crowdfunding. While some want to put a positive spin on this, like Kristopher Young, Founder and Executive Director of PROViDE, a non-profit that has had both success and failure in crowdfunding, who says, "If it is for a just cause, has been thought out and formalized, is sustainable (socially, economically, ecologically), it is a project or enterprise that can be perfect for crowdfunding." The implication, however, is clear: some projects aren't a good fit.

Here are some keys:

Social engagement: As Chris Camillo notes, "Crowdfunding is social funding. If an enterprise does not have the wherewithal and bandwidth to properly engage its donors on a social level by communicating personal gratitude, campaign progress and ROI (or ROD - Return on Donation) - it puts its brand, customer relationships, and reputation at risk."

Existing nonprofits: Andrea Lo, notes that crowdfunding is "not great for nonprofits who are already fundraising all the time and think this is going to just unlock a new audience of donors. Not the case, unless you're doing new things like empowering your volunteers to more deeply engage, or are launching a campaign around a specific initiative."

Complex projects without visual appeal: According to Yasmine Rezai, VP Marketing and Campaign Strategist for Health Tech Hatch, "Social projects or enterprises that require extensive explanations or proof and that do not easily convert into a 1-2 minute visual pitch make it hard for the crowd to engage. Future backers need to be able to quickly and easily grasp what you are trying to accomplish and why you need their help to reach your goal."

Boring, limited and commonplace: Piers Duruz suggests that there are three kinds of projects that don't work well in crowdfunding: a) "Boring topics. (At least topics you can't think how to raise passions around)," b) "Projects whose scope is strictly limited to a very small geographic niche," and c) "Well known topics that people have largely grown weary of hearing about already, with no new angle."

There are things you can do to avoid crowdfunding mistakes:

Friends of friends: Yazmine Rezai suggests that you "Craft your pitch with a friend of a friend in mind. These are the people most likely to (1) open the link that your mutual friend has forwarded, (2) back your cause if they like what they see, and (3) forward to their friend if they love what they see. Consider a $25 contribution level as the second of no more than six tiers of contributions and be sure that the reward is enticing to friends of your friends. If you are a banker planning to ask your banker friends to back your campaign once it's live, it's safe to assume that your banker friends have more friends that are bankers. If, on the other hand, you are an artist planning to ask your artist friends, then you should consider rewards that are enticing to other artists."

Marketing: David Boyce offers this advice, "The path to successful crowdfunding is through excellent marketing. Marketing, marketing, marketing. More marketing, better marketing, and more marketing again. And the key to marketing is to clearly define what is in it for the donor – why would she want to give to this campaign? Solving this puzzle effectively can help you convince lots and lots of donors to support your cause."

Create urgency: Boyce suggests that you "Create a time-constrained, project-based campaign, where the success of the campaign is measurable, and the project that gets funded as a result is observable. We have seen this work over and over among our customer base. Example: "Help us raise $50,000 so our school can open its doors." In cases where this urgency or specificity just isn't evident (like funding for research), you can manufacture the urgency by creating an event and recruiting people to participate: 'I'm running a 5K to help beat cancer. Help me meet my goal of raising $1,000 and support me on my run.'"

Be comfortable with "no": Andrea Lo points that you need to "Be comfortable with failure. Realize you have to work hard and get several No's before you get Yes's whether it is for press, large investment, or widespread support."

Raise money through traditional means first: David Boyce offers this final bit of advice, "Raise most of the money (at least 2/3) through traditional means first, then put the last bit out to the crowd to help "tip" the campaign. This is an effective strategy for many capital campaigns, ranging from churches to schools to universities. People like to be part of a winning team, and if the finish line is in sight it is easier to join in and help push the effort successfully across the finish line." Alex Budak, Co-Founder of StartSomeGood, agrees, advising you to "Invest time up-front in crafting your campaign and your marketing strategy. Though it's tempting to put all of your energy and focus solely in the days your campaign is live, refining your campaign, rallying your supporters and preparing a really strong outreach plan before you go live will allow you to start strong and position your campaign for success."

WHY CROWDFUNDING WILL EXPLODE IN 2013

This article appeared on Forbes.com (onforb.es/QJ0BQG) on October 12, 2012.

The world of entrepreneurial finance is changing rapidly; we are at a tipping point that will make what seems like a vibrant part of our global economy today seem small in one year's hindsight.

Whether you are a service provider, social entrepreneur, angel investor, venture capitalist, or one of the millions of people ready to become a small-scale start up financier, it is time to pay attention.

Estimates for annual crowdfunding transactions go as high as $500 billion annually compared to 2011's $1.5 billion (anticipated to be $3 billion in 2012). If crowdfunding even begins to approach that scale, it will completely change the landscape for start-up financing.

Sherwood Neiss, courtesy of Leverage PR

Jason Best and Sherwood Neiss helped lead the successful effort to get crowdfunding approved in the JOBS Act passed earlier this year. Niess explained that the folks at the SEC described themselves as "a reactive and not a proactive organization." The SEC explained that they needed direction from Congress before they could do anything about crowdfunding equity. "We delivered an act of Congress. They weren't expecting that."

The Act gives rulemaking authority to the SEC and FINRA; Best and Neiss are now meeting regularly with regulators to help define the shape of these rules—which could determine the success or failure of the Act.

According to Neiss, regulators approach novelty with a focus on preventing fraud—it's what they deal with every day. They aren't in the business of creating jobs—even though that is the legislation's intent.

Neiss explained that he and Best have helped to organize two groups to help frame the regulation and involve the people who will be most impacted by it: the Crowdfunding Professionals Association and the Crowdfund Intermediary Regulatory Advocates.

Neiss and Best recently wrote a piece for Venturebeat that explains the real issues that need to be resolved in the regulation. It is well worth the read.

WeSparkt founder Jonathan Blanchard explained WeSparkt's focus on social entrepreneurship. Their new crowdfunding platform is designed specifically to take advantage of the JOBS Act to allow social entrepreneurs focusing on a double bottom line (profit and social good) to raise equity.

Blanchard sites a Monitor study suggesting that crowdfunding will grow to $500 billion annually. His site will target impact investors hoping to create social change.

Fam Mirza, a young entrepreneur who has never let convention get in the way of a good idea, has launched a new watch company called 1:Face Watch that is a for profit business that promises to donate a portion of its revenue to one of six causes—each one associated with a color (think bright pink for breast cancer). I bought a white watch, feeding 16 people via One Day's Wages.

The watch is being sold through crowdfunding site Indiegogo, a popular crowdfunding site for social entrepreneurs. Mirza hopes to use the site as a launch pad, eventually allowing him to get the watch into the traditional retail channel.

Tim Harrington, CEO of FiPath, an independent financial planning web site, has created what it calls "College Registry," a tool for crowdfunding college savings. Families are encouraged to invite family and friends to donate to their kids' college funds rather than buy them gifts that will soon break. Not a bad idea in a world where four years at Princeton could cost $300,000 in 18 years.

Judy Robinette, a Partner at Crowdfund Capital Advisors, Neiss and Best's firm, noted that there are presently 700 different crowdfunding companies in development. This is quickly becoming a crowded landscape.

Javan Van Gronigan, founder of Donate.ly, is creating a new funding platform for social entrepreneurs that focuses on the contributors' ability (in this case, not investors) to invest directly in specific projects and track the use of the funds to its intended purpose on the ground. This would be in contrast to making an unrestricted donation to an organization that might then use the money for administrative costs.

Daniel Hirsh and Simon Erblich are trying to get a jump on crowdfudning with IPO Village. Using this open platform, they hope to complete their first crowdfunded initial public offering before the end of the year. They hope that by using a crowdfunding approach for an IPO for a tiny company that they can help the company avoid the death spiral financing patterns of other micro-cap, bulletin board and pink sheets' financings. IPO Village takes no fees, creating the hope for a more efficient capital raising process for tiny companies. The IPO is being conducted under existing regulations regarding IPOs and not under new JOBS Act regulations. The registration statement for the first company being put forward is not yet effective; it will be interesting to see if it is approved with the creative new approach for an offering.

Joy Schoffler of Leverage PR, speaking for IPO Village, explained their objectives this way: IPO Village is "democratizing access to IPOs."

12 SECRETS FOR SUCCESS IN CROWDFUNDING FOR SOCIAL ENTREPRENEURS

This article appeared on Forbes.com (onforb.es/T5eUmm) on November 15, 2012.

This week I've polled a variety of people with experience in crowdfunding to identify the secrets for success for social entrepreneurs. I've talked to people who've tried to raise money using crowdfunding and have raised absolutely nothing. Others have been blown away by the generosity of their friends, neighbors and social network, raising more than they hoped or expected.

Nathaniel Houghton, Congo Leadership Initiative

The following insights may help you to join the ranks of those who are blown away by the generosity of crowdfunders:

Start before your start: Nathaniel

Houghton, Founder and CEO of the Congo Leadership Initiative, notes that, "A successful campaign should have at least 50-60% of funds committed before the campaign launches." Sherwood Neiss, Principal at Crowdfund Capital Advisors and a leader in the JOBS Act effort to allow for equity crowdfunding, adds that you should vet "the idea with your crowd prior to going live so they can start coming in with funds ASAP."

You're in the movies now: Neiss notes that the video that introduces your campaign is vitally important. "Make a video that sells you and the idea within 2 minutes," he says. Megan Doepker, Founder of UNA Fashion, says, "Bring on the passion! Your campaign video is the vital tool to let your passion and vision shine through."

Be creative: Javan Van Gronigen, Co-Founder of Donately and Founder of Fifty & Fifty, suggests that a key to success is "be really creative and make something that is shared solely for its uniqueness."

It takes money to make money: Van Gronigen adds that you need "to put money behind a good campaign so you can do the grunt work to make it successful (emails, phone calls, web work, etc.)."

Leverage your social network: Neiss offers the counsel that represents the long pole in the crowdfunding tent: "Have a strong social network." Of those I surveyed for this article, only about 20% felt you could raise more than $2 per person in your social network. If you only have 78 Facebook friends and you've never understood what Twitter is for, building a successful crowdfunding campaign will be a challenge.

Support your supporters: Van Gronigen suggests that social entrepreneurs need to "come along side their fundraisers to cheer them on." Houghton add that "The most important thing is to make it easy for supporters to share the campaign with their contacts. Writing out emails and social media communications for their use makes it possible to grow the campaign organically through existing supporters."

Organize your campaign: Joy Schoffler, Principal of Leverage PR and who previously engaged in raising capital for startups, suggests organizing your list into As, Bs, and Cs, where the As are the "low hanging fruit." "If I could raise 25% from my A list I knew chances were good that the B's and C's would close the rest," she says.

"Tell a great story:" Alex Budak, Co-Founder of StartSomeGood, says, "Remember to tell your potential supporters why you're doing this in the first place. Why are you dedicating your life to this issue? Why are you giving up sleep and a traditional career to make a difference in this manner? Speak to your vision and your impact, and don't forget to connect with supporters on a personal level. Let your passion and your personality show through. Ultimately your ability to tell a compelling story and connect with your community will drive your success," he concludes.

"Again and again!" Doepker suggests that, "You need to engage your family, friends, social network, media and influencers in your industry. Be sure to include a call to action and why backing your campaign matters. For example, back UNA Fashion [on Indiegogo] to make a style statement and change the world through the movement to 'fashion the change!'"

Expertise, traction and scale: Rory Eakin, Co-Founder of CircleUp, notes that, "We find the most successful entrepreneurs are able to demonstrate three things for potential investors: expertise, traction, and potential to scale."

It takes work: Howard Orloff, Managing Director and Mayor of IPO Village, "The effort and resources put in to creating [and] promoting the campaign cannot be overestimated. The greatest idea or business concept can easily be lost in a poorly presented campaign."

Public relations: Simon Erblich, Founder of IPO Village, observes that, "From experience, we have found that retaining a PR firm familiar with the industry can be extremely worthwhile if you land the right firm... do your due diligence!"

A consistent theme from across the panel was that it is difficult to predict outcomes. Few campaigns gain "viral" traction, meaning that by and large crowdfunding is really "peerfunding." While Houghton suggested having half of the money for the campaign raised before it begins (see number one above), most were a bit more optimistic and several refused to suggest a number. Virtually all agreed that having a big, fast start was key to the long-term success of the campaign.

EIGHT CROWDFUNDING SITES FOR SOCIAL ENTREPRENEURS

This article appeared on Forbes.com (onforb.es/TIYyij) on September 10, 2012. The story did not list Fundly.com and should have. The story is reprinted here as it was originally posted.

If money is the only thing stopping you from doing something good in the world, stop waiting and start doing some good!

Nothing better symbolizes entrepreneurship than fundraising. Social entrepreneurs are no different. Today, there are a host of on-line resources for crowdfunding that social entrepreneurs can use to fund their projects, films, books, and social ventures. Today, I'll briefly profile eight.

Kickstarter.com: Kickstarter is the 800 pound gorilla in crowdfunding, originally designed and built for creative arts, many technology entrepreneurs now use the site, some reporting to have raised millions of dollars. The Kickstarter funding model is an all-or-nothing model. You set a goal for your raise; if your raise exceeds the goal, you keep all the money, otherwise your supporters don't pay and you don't get anything. This protects supporters from some of the risk of your running out of money before your project is completed.

StartSomeGood.com: StartSomeGood, which I used to raise some money for my book, Your Mark On The World, is great for early-stage social good projects that are not (yet) 501(c)(3) registered nonprofits. StartSomeGood uses a unique "tipping point" model for fundraising, allowing you to set a funding goal and a lower "tipping point" at which your project can minimally proceed and where you will collect the money you raise.

Indiegogo.com: Indiegogo allows you to raise money for absolutely anything, using an optional "keep what you raise" model with higher fees or pay less to use an all-or-nothing funding approach.

Rockethub.com: Rockethub is also a broad platform targeting "artists, scientists, entrepreneurs, and philanthropists" on their site, using a keep-what-you-raise model that rewards you for hitting your funding goal (or penalizes you for failing to hit it).

Pozible.com: Pozible, run from Australia, has a global platform for all types of projects, emphasizing "creative projects and ideas" and specifically precludes fundraising for charities. Pozible operates with an all-or-nothing funding model.

Causes.com: Causes is designed specifically for 501(c)(3) registered nonprofits to raise money. The fees are low and all donors on the site understand that all of the contributions will be tax deductible. Causes is widely used to launch "action" campaigns, like boycotts, petitions and pledges rather than fundraising campaigns.

Razoo.com: Razoo boasts that it has now helped 14,000 causes raise over $100 million. This site is exclusively for social good causes but is not limited to 501(c)(3), using a keep-what-you-raise model, charging just 2.9% of money raised.

Crowdrise.com: Crowdrise is a site for 501(c)(3) charities to raise money, with the novelty being that anyone can sign up to volunteer to launch a fundraising campaign for a charity already registered on the site. Everyone can instantly become a social entrepreneur for a cause they believe in.

All of these sites are making great things happen for real people every day, advancing the arts, entrepreneurship and philanthropy in myriad ways. Check them all out and decide which one is the best for you.

Note that in general, the tax deductibility of donations made on these sites is determined by the tax status of the organization to which you donate and not by the crowdfunding site used. Donations made through any of the sites to a 501(c)(3) registered nonprofit will generally be tax deductible for U.S. donors who itemize deductions on their tax returns. Check with your tax accountant if you have questions before you make a donation.

'KINGONOMICS' EMBODY THE SPIRIT OF SOCIAL ENTREPRENEURSHIP

This article appeared on Forbes.com (onforb.es/X8pZQL) on January 16, 2013.

Entrepreneur, religious leader, and author of Kingonomics, Rodney Sampson has long been a student of Martin Luther King. As a child he memorized King's "I Have a Dream" speech and was invited to perform the speech at local churches in Atlanta where he grew up. Kingonomics is Sampson's word for the economic principles (Sampson calls them "currencies") advocated by King.

Kingonomics by Rodney Sampson

These economic and entrepreneurial principles don't merely represent the economic principles and teachings of MLK, but more importantly, epitomize the spirit of social entrepreneurship in the 21st century.

Sampson recently hosted a conference for current and aspiring entrepreneurs in the Atlanta area and attracted top-flight entrepreneurs from around the country to come and present. (I was honored to be included in the roster of presenters; this provided me an opportunity to learn more about Sampson and his economic principles first hand.)

Kingonomics identifies the following twelve economic and entrepreneurial principles:

Service: More than customer service, Sampson advocates service to mankind, "Many of us are discovering that selfishness, the currency of greed, is not all it was cracked up to be in business school," he says.

Connectivity: "Dr. King was, above all, a champion of connectivity. By that I mean he was always looking to build community—physically, spiritually, mentally, emotionally, and economically," Sampson says.

Reciprocity: This principle represents a variation on the "buy local" theme with which we are all familiar. The key is to strategically give back to the communities from which you draw your profits. As an example, Sampson specifically encourages black churches to hire local contractors to build their churches.

Positivity: "We are no longer obsessed with defeating the competition. We aim, instead, to be the best we can be while embracing competition as positive and necessary," Sampson says.

Personal Responsibility: King, himself, embodied Gandhi's counsel to "be the change you wish to see in the world." Sampson argues that "followers must lead by the choices they make every day; then the leaders will follow."

Self-Image: Sampson argues not for vanity, but for the brand of pride that is defined as self-confidence. "Dr. King was a deeply spiritual man who believed that people have deep and abiding worth, no matter whom they are or where they come from," he says.

Diversity: Sampson, who grew up in an African American community saw his own world expand exponentially when he attended Tulane University. "We must... diversify our decision-making process by purposefully seeking out those who aren't of our same ethnicity, religion, gender or social backgrounds," he says.

Character and Dignity: "Character, one's moral or ethical integrity, is one of our most precious business currencies of all, and we must earn it, spend it, and invest it wisely at every opportunity," Sampson says.

Dreaming: Sampson, channeling MLK, challenges everyone to dream big with an eye toward changing the world. "We must each write our own internal 'I Have a Dream' speech, not only for our businesses but for our lives and the world as well," he says.

Rodney Sampson

Openness and Transparency: Sampson observes that America's "old boys club" has, perhaps unintentionally, done great harm to women and minorities who are often excluded from networks that operate behind closed doors. "We must learn to openly acknowledge our differences, with honesty, grace, respect, and even humor, as we continue to explore our commonality," he says.

Creativity and Innovation: Sampson argues that creativity and innovation are inextricably linked to diversity and openness, that collaboration with others of different backgrounds will lead to better outcomes. "Innovation will be the lynchpin of success in the new Collaborative Era," he says.

Courage: Interestingly, Sampson equates courage with love, noting, "Every human transaction, at its deepest level, boils down to a choice between fear and love... To act with love is to act with courage. It is to refuse to allow fear to dictate our actions and decisions."

The book is an inspiring guide to doing business in a sustainable way. I recommend it to anyone interested in doing business better.

One final note: Sampson is a big advocate of crowdfunding. At the conference in Atlanta last weekend, he organized four panels of experts to talk about crowdfunding. Sampson recognizes that crowdfunding represents an open and transparent source of capital that is allowing women and minorities to not only raise money they couldn't before, but also giving them an entrée into the closed networks of angel investors and venture capitalists.

You may not have heard of Rodney Sampson before, but I predict you'll hear from him again.

ABOUT THE AUTHOR, DEVIN D. THORPE

Devin Thorpe thinks he is the luckiest person alive. After being "let go" from the best job he'd ever had—as the Chief Financial Officer of the multinational food and beverage company MonaVie—he and his wife ended up living in China for a year where he wrote Your Mark On The World and embarked on the career he'd always wanted and hadn't dared dream.

Now, as an author and blogger for Forbes Devin writes about the things that inspire him, mostly stories of people who are making a positive difference in the world and how we can all be more like them. His current life isn't much like his past. As an entrepreneur, Devin ran—at separate times—a boutique investment banking firm and a small mortgage company. He served as the Treasurer for the multinational vitamin manufacturer USANA Health Sciences years before becoming CFO for MonaVie.

Devin squeezed in two brief stints in government, including two years working for Jake Garn on the U.S. Senate Banking Committee Staff and another year working for an independent state agency called USTAR, where he helped foster technology entrepreneurship during Governor Jon Huntsman's administration.

Devin is proud to be a Ute, having graduated from the University of Utah David Eccles School of Business, which recognized him as a Distinguished Alum in 2006. He also earned an MBA at Cornell University where he ran the student newspaper, Cornell Business.

Today, Devin channels the idealism of his youth, championing social good, with the loving support of his wife, Gail. Their son Dayton is a PhD candidate in Physics at UC Berkeley (and Devin rarely misses an opportunity to mention that).

You can connect with Devin at yourmarkontheworld.com (bit.ly/xaxQti), on Twitter (bit.ly/RLwP0p) at @devindthorpe, on Facebook.com/YourMarkOnTheWorld (on.fb.me/18ZdPCA) and on Google+ (bit.ly/RLwJWt). Or just send him an email at devin@devinthorpe.com.

15482699R10096

Made in the USA
San Bernardino, CA
26 September 2014